FOLLOWING ENGLAND ABROAD

GLENN BECKETT

FOLLOWING ENGLAND ABROAD

GLENN BECKETT

First published 2014 by DB Publishing, an imprint of JMD Media Ltd, Nottingham, United Kingdom.

ISBN 9781780914176

Contents

This book is dedicated to Maureen, Natalie and Emily, who are my three special girls, and also to Mum and Dad, for first introducing me to the greatest sport in the world.

Preface

I still remember receiving the phone call, one early morning in the spring of 1998.

"Alright Beckett, how do you fancy coming to France for the World Cup? It'll be 120 quid each, which includes flights and a villa on the beach. Are you up for it?"

Of course I said yes straight away. I was completely skint at the time as I was pretending to study at university, but a week on the beach in the glamorous south of France, with a World Cup match thrown in for good measure, sounded bloody good to me. It also presented me with the chance to fulfil an ambition I'd had for a while, which was to watch the England football team play abroad.

I'd been patriotic for as long as I could remember. I'd always had the England shirts and the England tracky top as a kid and I was fully aware of the St George Cross flag, as opposed to the Union Flag, which just left me feeling rather flat.

In 1989, I had attended my first England home match at the old Wembley, as we demolished Poland 3–0 and I became hooked after that experience, despite a rather long and tedious National Express coach journey back up to Sheffield, my home city, after the game. I eventually rolled into bed at some ridiculous time in the early hours after that trip down south, but the game itself, the atmosphere, the flag waving and the banter with my friends were all addictive.

After that, I went to as many England home games as I could over the years, but I had never made it overseas to watch the team play, mainly because I simply didn't have the cash at the time. I'd been fortunate enough to watch my club team, Nottingham Forest, play Bayern Munich away in the UEFA Cup quarter-finals in 1996, but that was a very cheap trip and involved a very long coach journey, and I had decided that when I got the chance to watch England play abroad, I wanted to do it in a bit more comfort.

When Ant phoned me that day in March 1998, I was sat on the sofa in my decrepit student house in a horrible area of Wolverhampton (is there a nice area in Wolverhampton?) called Whitmore Reans, near Molineux. He was very persuasive, but he knew that I'd be up for it anyway, as I was still struggling to find a job as I approached the end of my studies and I needed some kind of grand celebration to top off three hard years of work and study at university. I couldn't really afford the trip, but 120 quid plus beer money was within reach if I budgeted carefully. I was also aware that England had a decent team back then and I felt that they had a decent chance of winning the trophy (don't laugh!) and so I had to be a part of it. I wanted to experience the thrill of watching my team, my country, play abroad in a World Cup Finals.

My earliest memory of watching England play in any tournament finals comes from the 1980 European Championships in Italy, when I was eight years old. I remember seeing England struggle to a 1–0 defeat against the host nation, though I remember feeling that we'd been rather unlucky. A plucky defeat of Spain still left us short though, as Belgium and Italy sneaked through ahead of us out of our group. The bad luck continued in the Spanish World Cup in 1982, as two 0–0 draws against Spain and (West) Germany were not quite enough for us to make the semi-finals. I remember sprinting home from Primary School in order to be sat on the sofa in time for kick-off for the France match in that same tournament, and that sense of excitement has never left me when it comes to following the national team, despite a continuous catalogue of disasters, near-misses, controversy, red cards, missed penalties, incompetent referees and sheer bad luck over the years, which I am sure you do not need me to remind you of. It's just too painful.

Anyway, by the summer of 1998, I was in my mid-twenties and I'd had enough of living and studying in Wolverhampton. It was time for a change. I eventually managed to acquire a new job in Bristol, so I spent a few weeks sorting out a new rental house down there, before returning to Sheffield to catch up with the boys at home. The World Cup was just about to start.

Since that time, I've got married, lived overseas, bought a house, had a couple of kids and all the rest, but whenever possible, I still have to find the time to sneak off to some far flung corner of the earth in order to cheer on the England team. I'm the kind of person who will cheer on an England team in any sport or any game, whether it's football, or hockey, cricket, rugby, athletics, badminton, tiddly-winks, or paper, scissors, rock. I've seen an England cricket team win The Ashes in Australia, but nothing will ever compare to what I imagine it will be like when the England football team finally, finally get their hands on a trophy again.

As you have picked up this book, I hope that you can gain some kind of vicarious pleasure from reading about the exploits of a bunch of England fans, as we follow the team abroad. This is a tale of travel, of hope, of laughs, of arrests, of friendships and of brilliant, shared experiences, all of which were accompanied by large quantities of beer. There was also some reasonable football being played in the midst of it all.

Chapter One

FRANCE 1998

So there I am, sat on the sofa with a big smile on my face. I'd just put the phone down after my conversation with Ant and my mind was already drifting towards thoughts of the Mediterranean, the south of France, the heat, the sun, the glamour, the girls in bikinis, the beer, the banter and of course, the World Cup. My flatmate Graham came thudding down the stairs as he was dying to use the loo.

"What's up with you? You look like you've just won the lottery."

"I'm off to France for the World Cup lad. My mate from Sheffield is booking it all later today. Result or what?"

"Jammy git," was his succinct reply. He then dashed off to relieve himself, hurtling past our living room wall posters of Kelly Brook, Dannii Minogue and The Wonderstuff. Students, eh?

Graham was a good lad, despite coming from the northern wastelands of Middlesbrough. He would join me on a number of foreign trips over the years, to places such as Prague, Sydney, Berlin and Kiev. He was very proud of supporting Middlesbrough, though as they had never actually won anything at the time, I was never entirely sure why. He'd been in a relatively bad mood for a few days actually, because his Boro team had just lost 4–0 to my Forest team in a crucial promotion encounter at The City Ground. He'd also recently split up with his Norwich supporting girlfriend and he kept asking me if I thought he'd made the right decision in splitting up with her. I had to be honest, so I said she was a top bird and a good laugh, so no, I wasn't really willing to back his decision. To Graham's credit though, he'd always had a good taste in music, didn't mind a beer or three and he loved his football, so we got on.

I heard the front door open and slam, and in walked another of our flatmates, French Nick. I really respected the lad because he'd moved over to England from Nantes to try and improve his English, which was in need of some sharpening and refinement. He played in a band and had a decent CD collection, along with a sharp sense of humour, so again, we got on. He'd recently started working in a bar in Wolverhampton town centre, purely to try to improve his understanding and awareness of the vagaries of the English language. Graham and I had gone in to see him at work the night before, mainly to take the piss of course, as well as hoping to blag the odd free drink off him. The bar he'd chosen to work in was probably not the best choice in the world if he wanted to improve his language skills, as it was one of those places where the 'thump, thump, thump' dance music was played far too loud, so that you couldn't hear yourself think, never mind speak. On more than one occasion, we watched Nick struggle to understand a customer's order, but I couldn't help admiring his courage to even take the job on.

As Nick walked into our living room that Saturday morning, he greeted us by telling us about an exciting event he had witnessed whilst walking home from work late last night. He kept going on about a 'blue-job' that he had seen outside the bar, down a quiet side street. Graham and I looked at each other in a nonplussed way, not for the first time, whilst trying to figure out what Nick was attempting to describe. It was only when Nick mentioned that the man was standing up whilst the lady was bending down that we got the perfect picture in our heads. After about two minutes of laughing and tears, we set Nick straight about the pronunciation of this particular technique.

I mentioned to Nick that I was heading out to France for the World Cup and he seemed almost as excited as I was. He came from Nantes, which was in the North West of the country, whereas we were heading down to the South Coast, which was a fair jaunt from his neck of the woods. Nevertheless, he promised to visit us and help us with the language, providing I bought him a few beers. As if we would need that kind of help! My French GCSE skills were still there, in the back of my brain, somewhere.

A few weeks later I headed back up to Sheffield on the train. As a skint student, I'd perfected the art of making the journey without paying. I'd get the train from Wolverhampton down to Birmingham New Street station and sit comfortably on a seat without a ticket, because I'd noticed over time that the ticket inspectors didn't bother checking tickets before Birmingham as there were always masses of passengers getting on there, so they'd always wait until after New Street before making their way through the train. Once in Birmingham I then had to change trains and get the express up north. This proved more problematic as the journey was around 80 minutes, so the only way to make it for free was to hide in the toilets. Every time the train arrived at a different station, I'd hop out of the loo and move along into the next carriage, before hiding away again. It never failed! At the time, they didn't have ticket barriers at Sheffield station, so I could just saunter through easily, without any hassle from a jobsworth official. I know that it wasn't right, but some students have so little money that they have to save whatever they can for the occasional beer or three!

I was greeted by a few of my old mates when I walked into the local pub in Stocksbridge, which was called The Miners Arms. Nobody ever called it that by the way. It was known colloquially as 'The Rag', but to this day, I have no idea why. This pub, although plain and far from grand, was the setting for many a night out in my late teens and early twenties. It would also become almost like a meeting room for future England away trips featuring several of the local lads. The old landlord Steve always used to joke that if we stopped going in there he'd go out of business. Anyway, once reacquainted with the lads I happened to mention that I was off to France for the World Cup and that Ant was organising the trip. Upon hearing this information, the lads all burst out laughing.

"Coyney tours?" shouted Woody. "You'll all end up sleeping in a cave on the beach again!"

This was a worry, I must admit. You see, Ant was one half of the infamous Coyney Tours Company, along with his brother Matt. Not that this company actually existed, but it made for good banter in The Rag. The year before, Ant and Matt had booked a cheap last minute flight to Majorca and hopped on the plane with just 150 quid between them, along with a few basic necessities like a toothbrush and a change of underpants. They had no hotel booked, but as soon as they arrived they went out on a huge impromptu beer session. Somehow, they managed to blow all their money in the one night, and without anywhere to stay they decided to get some shut eye in a cave on the beach. They then had to beg, steal or borrow any food or drink they could until their mother could wire them some money through a few days later. What makes the story even funnier is that they were cut off from 'their' cave at certain times of the day because of the high tide.

The legend of Coyney Tours was there nibbling away at the back of my mind, but I somehow managed to keep the faith. Ant had promised "a villa right next to the beach that will sleep eight of us". I was prepared to give Coyney Tours a try, as I reasoned that this time, we'd have accommodation booked, plus I'd be in charge of my own finances. Most of the other lads in the pub could not be persuaded to join us in France at this time, but many of them would come on future trips watching England abroad as word spread over the coming years.

Despite Gazza being left out of Glenn Hoddle's squad for the World Cup, most England fans, including myself, felt that we had a strong team. There was no reason in my mind why we couldn't challenge strongly this time, on the back of a reasonably successful Euro 96 tournament in England. With players like Beckham, Scholes, Shearer and Owen, I was mildly optimistic as the opening match approached.

It all started badly from an England point of view, as television images and newspaper reports showed hooligans fighting and rioting in Marseille, the scene of England's opening game against Tunisia. The initial reporting seemed to place the blame on some English hooligans for starting the trouble, but it was only later that a different story emerged, which was that many locally based Algerian and Tunisian youths had been instigating confrontations in an aggressive manner, and some of our intellectually challenged morons decided to have a go back. Stories emerged of English fans having to barricade themselves in their hotel rooms, as gangs of knife wielding North African thugs attempted to cause maximum injury to anyone they suspected of being English.

Marseille has long been a place for North Africans to settle, as it is the main French port for those travelling from the former French colonies along the southern Mediterranean coastline. It is also a city plagued by crime, poverty, drugs and high unemployment. Whole pockets of the city are almost entirely Algerian or Tunisian enclaves, with many of these people living in abject poverty, with little hope and poor levels of education. Many of these people were fully behind the Tunisian team and hoped they would make an impact in the World Cup, so that they could temporarily forget their daily problems. When thousands of England fans arrived, with their reputation for hard drinking and extremely vocal support, many of the locals did not take too kindly to them. It all went pear shaped on the streets for a couple of days and I was glad to be in Sheffield, as opposed to Marseille's hard streets. My mate Jonny, who lived in France, confirmed that Marseille was, in his words, "a shithole".

England won the game against the Tunisians 2–0 without too much trouble, but I remember my mother questioning my decision to go out there a couple of days later. We were heading out to see the England v Romania game, which was taking place in Toulouse, a long way from Marseille. I must admit that apprehension had crept in a little bit, but I brushed it to one side whenever conversations in The Rag turned back to the trip. The local Sheffield lads making the journey were Ant, Matt, Deano and myself, along with four other friends of Matt who I didn't know.

I arrived at Luton airport ready for the flight to Carcassonne already feeling knackered. Luton is a long drive from Sheffield, and when you're getting picked up at 2.00am it does tend to play havoc with your sleep patterns. Ant's battered old Vauxhall Corsa had pulled up at the top of the driveway with Matt in the passenger seat and Deano in the back. I squeezed in alongside Deano after brushing an empty cigarette packet onto the floor. I was ankle deep in empty cans, bottles and fag packets, which was normal for any journey in Ant's car. It never seemed to occur to him that cleaning it out might be a plan. Ant drove fast, right elbow stuck out of the window whilst chain smoking with his left hand. It really was that kind of journey. Fortunately, the M1 behaved for once, as it should at that time of night, and we parked up at Luton Airport car park in plenty of time.

My body was craving coffee, but the other boys were having none of it. They dragged me to an airport bar, where we relaxed and waited for the other boys to arrive from different parts of the country. Andy, Mark and Martin arrived together, looking a lot more alert than I felt. They were all university friends of Matt and they all played together in a band called 'Enderby', which they had formed in Manchester a couple of years previously.

Matt was a very amusing bloke who had a way with words. Need a one liner? See Matt. Need a quick put down? See Matt. He was also the singer in the band and was ably supported by the rest of them. Andy and Mark were both extremely skinny and looked like they needed a decent meal or three, whereas Martin was shorter and stocky. Martin was the drummer in the band and also spoke fluent French, which we imagined would be of great use once we were over the channel. Sadly, he was a Derby County supporter, so I felt obliged as a Nottingham Forest fan to give him some friendly abuse, as they are our eternal rivals. The last one to arrive was Don, a tall chap who really was rather posh, certainly compared to the rest of us. What a motley crew!

We almost missed the Ryanair flight as we got a bit too carried away in the bar and we managed to lose Matt, who had gone to "drop the kids off at the pool" in the toilet, but he couldn't find his way back to the same bar he had left just ten minutes earlier. Fortunately, we tracked him down at the departure gate and got on the Carcassonne flight. The reason we were flying there was basically because a flight to Toulouse, the match venue, would have been expensive and anyway, Coyney Tours had booked this supposed "majestic villa, right on the beach, with a sea view" near a small coastal town called Gruissan, which was much closer to Carcassonne than any other airport. The flight arrived in France without any problems and we headed out to the taxi rank once we'd collected our bags.

Martin took it upon himself to sort out two taxis for us, which was the first time his French came in useful. I mean, I had a decent French GCSE and knew that I could hold my own with the local lingo, but Martin could actually hold decent conversations and we figured that his linguistic abilities might help to stop us from being ripped off. We only found out later that we could have caught the train to Narbonne from Carcassonne, before paying for a short taxi ride from there. We certainly did just that for the return journey, saving us a fortune in the process.

The taxi driver was a grumpy, miserable sod who didn't seem to enjoy his work. He spoke pigeon English and declared his disdain for the round ball game, as he was very much a rugby man. He didn't have any interest in the World Cup whatsoever and it reminded us of the fact that most people in this south-west corner of France did tend to prefer men with odd shaped balls. It wasn't the kind of excitable, carnival-like atmosphere I had been expecting to find on arrival.

We got dropped off at our accommodation and I was somewhat

underwhelmed to find myself in what looked like a small car park surrounded by minute townhouses and chalets.

"Where's this beach facing villa then Ant?" I said, unable to resist a slight dig at the tour organiser.

"Buggered if I know mate," he replied with a laugh.

Martin and Ant set off to find any building that vaguely resembled a reception, while the rest of us waited in the car park. I noticed a huge cockroach climbing up a wall, which must have been about half the size of my hand. The sun was hot and we were all knackered, so we sat down in some shade and waited for the boys to return.

After about five minutes they returned, with Ant gleefully swinging a large key ring around his forefinger. He led us down an alley in between two apartment blocks and sure enough, there in front of us, was the sea. Well, kind of. The sea itself was a kilometre or so away to the right of us, whereas what we had in front of us was just a shallow inlet of water, separated from the Mediterranean by a large sand bank across the bay.

Our 'villa' resembled a modernised terrace house, with two storeys, a small front yard and lots of grey render. It wasn't unattractive, but it hardly took your breath away. As we entered and explored, we noticed a tiny kitchen area to the right, a small laundry room to the left, one double bedroom downstairs, along with a small shower room, and one bedroom with bunk beds upstairs.

"How is this villa supposed to sleep eight people?" commented Don incredulously.

Ant just laughed again. "Well, I suppose two could share the double bed, and we can get six on the bunks upstairs, at a push", he suggested, rather too ambitiously. Deano and I started edging closer to the downstairs bedroom, hoping that the others wouldn't notice. We were the only non-smokers on the trip and it was close to the toilet, which was an important consideration, taking into account all the beer that was probably going to be consumed over the next week! We edged a bit closer then chucked our bags on the bed and 'claimed' it. This proved to be a good move over the next few days, as stumbling into this bed late at night would require far less control than trying to navigate the stairs to the five bunk beds.

Some of us hurriedly unpacked and quickly put on some shorts, eager to get out and explore. I grabbed a bottle of sun cream, knowing that our (mostly) northern English skin would burn easily outside. We had a look around and noticed little in the way of immediate facilities, other than a tiny little shop and a small bar. Needless to say, we all headed into the bar to check it out. The tables were all white and plastic, with uncomfortable red chairs surrounding them. To describe the decor and furniture as basic would be somewhat of an understatement. However, they did sell Kronenbourg 1664!

It was around lunchtime by this time, so we had a few thirst quenchers before getting stocked up with some supplies at the shop. It sold very little, but it was enough to keep our fridge loaded with beer, bottled water, cheese, ham, eggs, toilet rolls and bread. The checkout girl was also extremely attractive, with a very flirtatious smile, but sadly, she couldn't speak a word of English. Not that it would stop a few of us from trying to befriend her over the next few days of course!

We decided we'd better check out Gruissan town itself, which left us with two options: either to walk along the busy main road which went slightly inland, or promenade along the beach. No contest. We applied the factor 30, then set off along the beach, which was really nice, despite the sand burning our feet. After a couple of minutes we walked right past a couple of girls who were playing a topless game of volleyball over a net. We must have all been obviously staring, as they both giggled a "bonjour" to us, which was a greeting we heartily returned with enthusiasm! You didn't tend to get those kind of views in Sheffield. Well, not outside anyway!

Gruissan was a beautiful little town at the water's edge, with lots of old stone houses which gazed out at the Mediterranean Sea. There were lots of cafes, bars and restaurants with a sea view and the place had a nice, relaxed vibe about it. The only thing that was missing was any kind of World Cup fever! We couldn't see a single flag or poster advertising the fact that arguably the world's biggest sporting tournament was taking place in the country, right now. The locals seemed content enough to meander through the streets, sit at cafe tables sipping on a café-au-lait, or simply sat at the water's edge, looking at the view, and to be honest, who could blame them? It was a really attractive place which compared more than favourably to grey old Wolverhampton, where I'd just spent three years, supposedly studying.

We watched the afternoon kick-off game back in the local resort bar, before going down to the beach for a kick about. The beach itself was perfect for football, as it was reasonably flat and not too soft. We practised a few keepy-uppies but we had to stop as Ant and Andy were so bad. It was far easier to challenge some local lads we spotted playing nearby, so before we knew it, we had a full-on France versus England match on the beach, which ended up being an excellent contest which we just shaded, thanks to our overtly physical approach! I even managed to score with an overhead scissors kick, which was something I didn't let the rest of the lads forget for the rest of the week.

It was just turning dark by the time we left the beach, so after a quick shower we headed back to the local bar as we were all exhausted at the end of Day One and we couldn't be bothered to head back into Gruissan. After far too many Kronenbourgs we headed off back to the 'villa', but not before Deano, Matt and Andy had treated us to a game of 'Hide the wheelie bins,' which involved dragging several wheelie bins behind them as they walked, before re-positioning them outside someone else's house. Very helpful lads!

The next morning I was up and in the kitchen, making a badly needed coffee. I heard footsteps, so I turned around to see a dishevelled looking Ant stumbling down the stairs in his shorts and flip-flops, cigarette in hand, eyes red and blotchy.

"I tell you what, it's beer o'clock," he said with a wink. He went straight to the fridge and cracked open a can of Amstel. It was 10.00am.

"I can't believe what I'm seeing Ant," I replied. "You only stopped drinking a few hours ago! There's no way I could face a beer at this time of day. Just give me a coffee and a bacon and egg sandwich mate, and that's me sorted."

"Well, you've never really been known for your drinking prowess," laughed Ant.

"Yes, but I'd still like to have my own liver by the time I'm 40 mate," I replied. "Is anybody else up yet?"

"Yeah, Mark's stirring a bit. Mind you, that could be because of the odour I left behind up there!"

We discussed the scores from yesterday's games and then thought about the Romania match, which was now only two days away.

"Who would you have up front with Shearer?" I asked.

"Got to be Owen for me mate. I know he's young, but defenders are scared of speed aren't they?" he answered.

Ant was spot on, though you'd never know it if you'd ever seen him play. We played Sunday League together, along with lots of other lads who frequented The Rag at home. During one game, I'd sent him clean through on goal with a beautiful pass (if I do say so myself!) and he suddenly stumbled, lost his footing and collapsed in a heap, around the edge of the penalty area. The chasing defender laughed out loud and calmly collected the rolling ball before lashing it to safety. Ant proceeded to crawl on his hands and knees towards the touchline, before loudly vomiting. We'd had a big night out on the Saturday, when, as usual, we'd all finished up at Sheffield's greatest night club, The Leadmill. After just a few hours sleep, Ant had woken up, had a can of Coke, bought the 'Sunday Sport' to read (or should I say, to look at the pictures) and he felt that he was ready to perform. Or maybe not.

We ended up spending the day on the beach and then I had a nice surprise when French Nick turned up, as promised several weeks ago. He was staying further down the coast in Perpignan with his family, but my instructions were obviously good enough to follow as he'd made it here for a day. This was in the days before most people had mobile phones, so his appearance in itself had to be considered a success. Matt's mate 'Cheese' also turned up. He was a French based English lad who had a particular fondness for weed. He turned up with a huge bag of it and seemed to be permanently attached to his possession. The only time I'd ever seen as much weed in one place was on a television documentary. Every time I looked at Cheese, he was either smoking weed or preparing one for somebody else. It wouldn't have surprised me if he'd slept with that bag, because it was like an umbilical cord to him.

Later on in the evening, he took us to a bar called 'Le Tribord' in Gruissan, which just happened to be a Marseille supporters club bar for the region. The Marseille club badge was prominent inside and on the windows, so we just hoped the unfortunate events which had occurred in that city just a few days ago would not be held against us, on account of our nationality. We needn't have worried. Martin's silver tongue worked wonders on the pretty barmaid and we had Nick and Cheese helping us out anyway. Deano had his favourite brown shirt on, yet again, so we mercilessly took the piss, whereas Mark, Cheese and Andy seemed only interested in smoking as much weed as was humanly possible.

Later on in the evening we moved to a different bar and surprisingly, Ant took a shine to a local girl and they actually got talking. Ant was no Casanova, so I think we were all a bit surprised more than anything else. He was over in the corner talking to this girl for quite a while and he seemed perfectly happy.

"We'll see you back in The Tribord," announced Don, as the rest of us left him to it, due to the fact that the bar had no football on the TV.

In the Marseille supporters bar in the South of France.

After about three hours, there was still no sign of Ant, so of course we just laughed and presumed he'd got lucky. This is just how blokes are I suppose. If the roles were reversed, I'm sure that a bunch of girls would have been extremely concerned and probably wouldn't have even left their friend, but that's blokes for you.

We all went for a late night pizza at a restaurant down by the water that was just about to close. The moody waiter wasn't too happy to see us, but we did still manage to get served, due to more smooth talking in the native language from Martin. As we left, I somehow managed to get separated from the rest of the lads and without mobile phones, it was much harder to track them down. I had a bit of a look around and went back to both the earlier bars, but I couldn't see them. I decided to head for home as I was tired by that stage. I decided against the beach route, mainly because I knew it was hard work stumbling along the sand, so I headed for the main road, as I presumed it would be well lit. Well, it was, but only for the first 500 metres or so, and then it was sheer blackness. The road tapered away from the coast and behind some small hills as I struggled to see where I was going. You have to remember that I'd had a skinful of beer and wine by this time, so I needed all my wits about me to simply place one foot in front of the other. A couple of cars passed by and I was grateful for the shining headlights to be honest. After what seemed hours, but probably wasn't, I eventually located our 'villa' and walked in to find all the lads, except Ant, sat down and having a beer.

"What happened to you?" asked Matt with a chuckle.

"Well, I lost you lot and couldn't find you, so I just walked back and it took me bloody ages," I shrugged.

"We've been here about half an hour lad. We got a couple of taxis," said Deano. "He tried ripping us off, but Nick got angry and put him straight in no uncertain terms."

"Nice one Nick. Just for that, you can kip on the sofa," I replied with a laugh. "Any sign of Ant?"

"He'll be getting his end away," laughed Mark.

"Give over. This is Ant we're talking about," replied Martin. "What Ant knows about women can be written down on the back of a postage stamp," he added, not unfairly.

After a few more beers most people dropped off, with Nick the first to nod off. Andy the artist thought it would be amusing to draw a moustache and glasses on Nick's face with a permanent marker. A beard and the legend 'frog' were soon added, much to everyone's amusement.

The following morning, everyone congregated in the small kitchen area. There was still no sign of Ant.

At about midday, there was a loud knock at the door. Martin walked over to answer it and in walked Ant, looking very much the worse for wear.

"Good night then Ant?" I asked with a grin.

"Don't know what you mean Beck," he replied with that permanent smirk of his.

"Was she any good?" Deano wanted to know.

"I don't know what you're talking about," Ant again responded.

"Whatever lad. We saw you looking cosy all night, so don't deny it," his brother chuckled.

"OK, look, I was well in there I admit, I mean, it must have been pretty obvious I thought," Ant started off, "but it all went a bit pear shaped," he chuckled.

"What was her name?" enquired Mark.

"Clarissa."

"Go on," demanded Don.

"Well, I thought it was looking good, cos I'd given it the sweet talk and all that bollocks, as you do, and then she invited me back to her flat, which was about ten minutes walk away. I was rubbing my hands together, thinking I'd got a result. She led me in and gave me a drink, which I happily accepted, obviously," he laughed. "Anyway, we went through into the bedroom and I saw loads of photos of her and this bloke, loads of 'em, and he was enormous, I'm talking rugby player size. So I asked her who it was and she said it was her boyfriend, but that it was ok because he was away with friends for the night. She tried it on a bit, but to be honest I was thinking about bottling it then anyway, when he suddenly phoned her AND she answered. They were gibbering away in French so I've got no idea what they were talking about, but anyway, she then said I'd better leave! His night out had been a cock-up apparently, so he was on his way back. I was out of there like lightning lads, I tell yer."

"You should have brought her back here," suggested Don.

"Oh, yeah, right. This place is really romantic and smells nice with eight blokes in it, doesn't it," Ant countered. "Anyway, I just legged it basically, because I wasn't exactly sure how far away her bloke was. Thing is, I walked back into town, but I got lost and I didn't see any taxis anywhere. I only had about 30 Francs left on me anyway and I was knackered and pissed, so I sat down on this bench for a bit. Before you know it, I was gone. Kipping on a bench!"

"So, where have you been this morning?" asked Matt.

"Well, I only woke up a couple of hours ago and I was starving hungry and lost, so I bought myself a croque-monsieur (a type of cheese and ham toastie) and then tried to get my bearings. I was at the other end of town and it took me a while to get back to the beach. I've just walked on here now," he laughed.

"Bleedin 'ell lad," I said, "you were lucky you weren't mugged, or worse!"

On reflection, I was a fine one to talk as I'd done a similar thing myself about a year earlier in Wolverhampton. I'd been out in the Student Union bar having a great night out with friends. In those days, you could still get the classic 'Pound a pint' deals in those kinds of places, but I think I went a bit overboard, unless somebody spiked my drinks. I remember leaving the Union Bar on my own rather the worse for wear, and I decided to take a short cut home through the park. Then, there it was in front of me, looking very inviting and welcoming: a park bench. I laid down on it and within a very short time I was out like a light. It was approximately an hour later when my friend Dave happened to see me whilst he was taking the same short cut home, from the same bar.

Poor old Ant. We gave him grief about it for the rest of the day, as you would expect. We spent the majority of the afternoon on the beach, but then Don and Matt challenged each other to a swimming race across the bay outside our villa. The distance across to the other side was about 150 metres or so, and the amateur bookies amongst us ensured that bets were placed whilst the rest of us just chilled out and wound them both up in our front yard. Let's just say the result was inconclusive, so all cash was returned.

We thought we'd better be sensible for once that night, as the following day was going to be a big one, with an early start. We were off to Toulouse to see England's next World Cup game, against the skilful but beatable Romanians. We had a few beers in the local bar before getting some shut eye.

The alarm clock went off early and I groaned. The sound of an alarm clock is never a good one is it? Especially when you've got a hairy, red-headed bloke snoozing a few feet away from you.

"Go on Beckett, you get up first. I'll have another ten minutes lad," said Deano as he buried his head into the pillow.

If I ever did 'pull' on this trip, I'd need to think about how I would have to make sure that Deano stayed away, ideally in a pub, or outside on the floor perhaps, if he was open to bribery.

After downing a couple of coffees we left and walked around to the little shop, from where we phoned for a couple of taxis. We paid for the short journey to Narbonne and then went to the train station to buy return tickets to Toulouse. Even my French was up to scratch with these kind of chores, so it wasn't a problem. As we waited on the platform, I noticed just two other England fans, further along the platform, one of whom was wearing a Middlesbrough shirt. My old flatmate Graham would have been proud!

All ready for Toulouse and England v Romania!

For the first time on this trip, World Cup fever was really starting to take hold today. We were obviously all up for it and excited about what lay ahead, but it also helped that Narbonne station had made an effort, with lots of flags, posters and advertisements noticeably related to the tournament. The SNCF train arrived on time and we all climbed on board. We decided to try and get away with sitting in the First Class carriages as the train was quite full. If challenged, we decided that we could just play dumb, as innocent foreign tourists. Some of us were better at the 'playing dumb' part than others! We lasted about 20 minutes actually, before being politely requested to move along to cattle class. The journey was fine, as it only lasted for about an hour and a half, before we entered the suburbs of La Ville Rose, the pink city, otherwise known as Toulouse.

At this point, I should bring up the fact that none of us actually had match tickets for the game. We were naïve first time followers of England overseas and indeed most of our party hadn't even been to Wembley to see our national team play, with the exception being yours truly, on many occasions. Our plan was to simply blag some tickets on the day itself in Toulouse, whether that be from fellow fans, French cafe owners with spares, or if need be, from a ticket tout near the stadium. This kind of thing does happen, but I suppose it all depends on how deep your pockets are, especially when it comes to buying from touts. At that time, in 1998, most of us were students or ex-students and we certainly didn't have fat wallets in our pockets. Our attitude really was more akin to the old mantra, 'fingers crossed and hope for the best'.

The train pulled in at Toulouse station and we jumped off and practically sprinted along the platform in our eagerness to see some of the city, find some tickets and of course, enjoy the odd beer or six. As we walked around and explored over the course of the day, the city seemed to be a decent enough place, though it didn't really have any spectacular buildings or obvious tourist attractions from what we saw. Having said that, we were only there for the day, but it seemed like a smart enough, medium sized city. Surprisingly, it even had an underground train network, which we occasionally used to get around, from one bar to another! It wasn't an especially big underground network, or 'metro' as they called it, but I can think of other far bigger cities, such as Sydney, which are really crying out for an underground network like this, in order to relieve the horrendous traffic congestion which affects that city, and others.

We spent a fair bit of time sat outside a couple of very pleasant bars, engaged in some banter with other English, French and Romanian fans that we met. A Romanian bloke walked past us with his videocam pointing in our direction, so I held up my fingers to predict the score for later that evening: 2–1. Little did I know how right (and wrong) I would be.

It was an overcast, cloudy day and a little bit cooler than recently, so for some reason, we thought these weather conditions would be an advantage for England. I suppose we were being what we might term 'typical' England fans, clutching at straws, as we were desperate, simply desperate for the team to perform how we believe they can and should.

Our search for tickets was proving fruitless as well. No cafe or bar staff had any spare tickets, nor knew of anyone who may have had some. No England fans had spares either and in fact quite a lot were in a similar boat to us, just simply hoping to acquire one, from someone, somewhere. The problem with Toulouse's stadium, the Stade Municipal, was that it was just too small for an England match and the associated large demand for tickets. At a little over 35,000, we felt it was a bit small for a huge World Cup game involving two European nations, even though Romanian supporters were few and far between back then.

About two hours before kick-off and still without tickets, we overheard a very angry conversation which we muscled in on. We were just walking between bars on the Rue du Tourneux, when a group of shocked England supporters informed us that a tabloid 'journalist' from a popular red top newspaper back in England, had just offered them 200 quid if one of them would throw a brick or a bottle at a cafe which had a handful of Romanian supporters sat outside it. After they'd got over the initial shock, they'd almost lynched the cretin and told him where to go, in no uncertain terms. Unbelievable stuff! I'd always distrusted the tabloids, as I felt they were far more interested in sensationalism and scandal than the welfare and actual progress of the England team in tournaments. This incident just backed up my suspicions and all of us felt outraged and repulsed that an individual acting on behalf of a popular so-called 'newspaper' could stoop so low as to try to tarnish the reputation of his own country, in front of the world's media, by attempting to instigate a violent incident, especially after what had just gone on in Marseille only a few days before. What an incredibly stupid way to earn a living. It starts to make you think about how other violent incidents around football matches in the past may have been started off, especially when certain newspapers seem to come up with lots of on-the-spot photographs of aggressive and disorderly fans misbehaving in a violent way. Why might they do that? The thought still staggers me to this day. One very famous Sunday newspaper recently went out of business after a different kind of scandal and I for one shed absolutely no tears at all. Some of the so-called journalism prevalent in our tabloid newspapers is utter garbage and I despair at the motivations of the editorial teams and journalists on such publications. It does seem to me, on some occasions, that the antics of certain newspaper journalists seem to suggest that they actually want the England football team to fail. Why else would they create or search for stories that can only have a negative effect? They also seem to deliberately print negative stories just as a tournament is about to start! Why can't they hold off with scandalous alleged news stories until a tournament is over and done with? That's the British tabloid press for you. Not all journalists and news editors are of that ilk, but it appears that too many are.

We had another quick drink and then started to walk towards the stadium, known as The Stade Municipal. Our hopes of acquiring match tickets were disappearing down the drain, along with some tabloid journalist's morals. We continued to ask fellow fans and lots of locals, but we got nowhere. As we came closer to the proximity of the stadium, we noticed several ticket touts at work, and without a word of a lie, they were all Scousers! It felt like we were suddenly extras in a production of '*Bread*' or '*The Liver Birds*' as we heard their familiar, but amusing, high pitched tones, as they tried to buy or sell tickets. "Any spaaiire tihhkkkets?"

Sadly, they all seemed to want between 400 to 500 quid per ticket, which was way out of our price range. I mean, I think we all expected to have to pay a bit over the odds, but those prices were outrageous. There was no way we could afford it, being skint students, or recently ex-students. The realisation that we weren't going to get into the stadium was a huge blow, as that was after all, the focal point of the trip. We sat down for a while on some grass, feeling collectively gutted.

"Come on gentlemen, chin up," offered Don. "We might as well go back to that last bar and try and get a decent seat in front of the tv, before it gets too packed. There's nothing we can do about it now, unless we're all able to shell out 500 beer tokens each to get in."

We all knew that he was right, but it was such an anti-climax. The feeling of disappointment and frustration was almost tangible. Wearing resigned expressions on our faces, we trudged back towards a decent looking bar we'd been in earlier. There was still about half an hour to go before kick-off, but the bar was absolutely heaving already. The vast majority of the patrons inside appeared to be England fans, who may well have had a similar experience to us. There were a handful of locals in as well, but I didn't notice any Romanians.

We settled on a corner spot inside the bar with a table, close to the wide screen television, whilst Matt got the beers in. I was so annoyed and frustrated. I'd been watching England at Wembley for several years and I thought this was going to be the first time I'd get to see them play overseas, thereby fulfilling an ambition. Watching Forest play away at Bayern Munich in 1996 was a superb experience and I was hoping for more of the same here, but with a larger group of friends.

The game itself was a disaster. England played reasonably well, but they couldn't seem to turn the screw and create enough opportunities. I felt that it was just a matter of time until our midfield got hold of the ball and started to direct and dominate, but it never seemed to really happen. Anderton, Batty, Scholes and Ince didn't really get on top of the opposition enough, though I felt Shearer and Sheringham up front would get the goals if opportunities came their way. Disaster struck on 47 minutes, as Viorel Moldovan put the Romanians in front after a slip from Tony Adams. England manager Glenn Hoddle replaced Teddy Sheringham with a young Michael Owen shortly afterwards, and he came up with the goods on 79 minutes. Shearer played the ball back across the edge of the six yard box, Scholes got a slight touch, and then to our delight, Owen smashed the ball into the back of the net from close range to make it 1–1. The bar went crazy, with frustrated Englishmen (and women) jumping up and down in delirium and ecstasy. Ant and I were screaming in each other's faces, yelling and cheering, as we briefly lost the plot.

What could and should have been an acceptable draw soon turned into an abysmal defeat, as once again, England proved capable of cocking it up, big time. Graeme le Saux failed to clear a long ball and Dan Petrescu slid in from the left hand side to steer the ball past David Seaman, inside his near post, in the very last minute of the game. Somebody, somewhere in the bar smashed a glass in frustration, but we were all too stunned to speak. The whole bar was suddenly littered with expletives, as fellow long suffering England fans, frequently used to disappointment, let go of their innermost thoughts.

So, that was it. A 90th minute goal sentenced us to a 2–1 defeat in a game that should never have been lost. The French bar staff appeared sympathetic, even if they were just acting (with self-preservation in mind!) and we all stumbled out into the street. The walk back to the train station was a long one, but the crowd of England fans walking the same route seemed understandably gutted, so there was little sign of any joie de vivre.

There wasn't really much to say, beyond the obvious. As football fans, we'd all been there before. Losing to a last minute goal isn't nice, but the disappointment is magnified several times when it happens to you overseas after spending a great deal of money you don't have!

The late train back to Narbonne was absolutely packed and we had to cram in like sardines in a tin. There were no available seats anywhere, so we ended up standing the whole way back, which wasn't ideal as we were all exhausted and mentally drained. The train itself was heading south to Barcelona and most England fans we chatted to were actually staying on the Costa Blanca or the Costa Brava, across the border in Spain. They had much further to go than we did and most of their facial expressions reflected this. Ant found a space on the floor and pulled his knees up to his head and attempted to get some sleep. The rest of us just worked through the post-mortem and discussed the well known failings of the England football team. Should Beckham and Owen have been on from the start? Should Le Saux have managed to get rid of that dangerous ball in the last minute? Should Seaman have saved it? Why weren't we able to dominate possession?

Most of the next day was spent sleeping, relaxing and recovering from the previous day. I resolved to try this kind of experience again though, but next time, I knew I had to make sure I had match tickets. The camaraderie and banter amongst the boys had been brilliant, but not managing to get into the ground and losing the game had taken the shine off it a bit by the end of the trip. One year later, I did manage to improve upon the experience of following England abroad.

Chapter two

BULGARIA 1999

By 1999, I was still living in Bristol and I was enjoying my job. I was working for a finance company in the north of the city and I was sharing a house in Bishopston, just across the road from the Gloucestershire County Cricket Ground. Bristol is a great city to live in and I still have many fond memories of the place, including the quirky local accent!

When the draw was made for the qualifying rounds of the Euro 2000 Championships, England were grouped with Sweden, Poland, Bulgaria and Luxembourg, which on the face of it, seemed a decent enough draw and one that England should have expected to qualify from. I had definite ambitions to drag some of the lads on an away trip after experiencing France 98, and the fixture that stood out for me was Bulgaria away in June, 1999. The fact that the match was scheduled for June was ideal, because it meant that the trip could again be made into a summer holiday, as well as a trip to watch a football match. Temperatures in Bulgaria were very agreeable at that time of year, especially along the Black Sea coast, and it was a country I had always wanted to visit, for a variety of bizarre and off the wall reasons.

As an eight-year-old kid, I had memories of my beloved Forest team being knocked out of the 1980–81 European Cup by the mysterious Bulgarian army team, CSKA Sofia, despite the fact that Forest were European Champions at the time. I also used to love my 'Top Trumps' card game as a child and for some reason, I remember being fascinated by a couple of the trains that came from Bulgaria. Sad I know, but bear with me on this. As a teenager, I developed an interest in Eastern Europe and all the stories and tales regarding the mysteries of the Iron Curtain and the communist states behind it, who were all influenced and manipulated by the Soviet Union. There was also the curious story of Georgi Markov, a dissident writer from Bulgaria who was murdered with a poisoned umbrella tip on Waterloo Bridge in London, during September 1978. He was allegedly murdered by the Bulgarian Secret Service, known as the DS (Darzhavna Sigurnost), though the actual identity of the murderer remains a matter for conjecture and debate. All these stories and more had given me a fascination for the country and I even joined the English-Bulgarian friendship society in the late 1990s.

Then there was the great Bulgarian team at the 1994 World Cup, in the US. They progressed all the way to the semi-finals before eventual defeat to Italy, but their quarter-final win over Germany captured the imagination of football fans everywhere, as the underdogs came from one down to beat the mighty Germans. The Bulgarian talisman Hristo Stoitchkov had equalised from a free-kick, before the balding Yordan Letchkov got the winner with a brilliant diving header. My favourite Bulgarian player from that team however, was the full-back Trifon Ivanov, otherwise known as Wolfman. He was built like a brick outhouse and had a beard to rival Brian Blessed or David Bellamy. His free-kicks amused me the most. Despite having the talented Stoitchkov in the team, Ivanov somehow got to take some of the free-kicks, and I swear that every free-kick he took was blasted miles over the crossbar into row Z, no matter where the free-kick was taken from. You could tell he was a tough guy though, because none of his team mates ever lambasted him after yet another of his pathetic attempts on goal.

I had been to Eastern Europe a few years before, when I had experienced the beauty and mystery of Croatia and Slovenia, and that visit had also whetted my appetite for more of the old Iron Curtain countries, which I found fascinating. Bulgaria in the summer time seemed too good an opportunity to miss out on, so I set about persuading the lads drinking in The Rag, whenever I went back up to Sheffield for a weekend. Matt, Ant and Deano were up for it again, which was a bonus, but we also acquired some new recruits for the planned Bulgarian adventure, namely Jim, Met and Scarecrow.

Jim used to play in the same Sunday League team as myself, which was called Rollneck Rings FC. The deal was that we had to name ourselves after a steel ring making company in Sheffield and they would then buy us our kit and cover the match fees, which seemed fair enough to us, even if the team name seemed a bit naff. My claim to fame in this team was that I scored 42 goals in the 1994–95 season, as centre-forward. Jim was a robust, commanding centre-half who took no prisoners at the back, though I have seen a few P&O cruise liners turn around quicker! Jim liked a beer or three and was another Sheffield Wednesday supporter, along with Deano, Matt, Met and Scarecrow. I was the only Forest fan on this trip as my brother 'Oz' was still pleading poverty at the time and couldn't afford to go. At least he'd make up for that in the future.

Met was an ex-rocker who used to have the whole long hair and pony tail thing going on, before he saw the light and cut it off. He was a funny, funny bloke, especially after a beer, but he'd be the first to admit that he had close to zero football talent on the park, which was just as well, because this trip would not require his mercurial talents with the ball at his feet, only those talents with a pint glass in hand. He had his stag do in Brighton a few years later and my brother and I thought it would be a good idea to try and shave his hair off, by way of celebration of course. What stopped us was the fact that we couldn't find a cordless shaver anywhere in Brighton as we moved and staggered between pubs in the afternoon. Fortunately for us, a few months after his wedding he decided to do it himself anyway and went for the peanut look!

Scarecrow was so-called simply because he used to have a haircut (and I use that term loosely) which seemed to be a hybrid version of Worzel Gummidge's hairdo and a bird's nest. By 1999, he was a much sharper individual, so we teased him constantly about his new 'boy band' look. Scarecrow took it all with good humour and promised to beat us on the pool table, as he fancied his talents with cue in hand. Like most of us, Scarecrow had a great taste in music and loved nothing more than going to gigs and concerts to see live bands. I had spent many an evening with him and most of the other lads doing just this. As another Sheffield Wednesday supporter, he wasn't used to seeing much quality football, so I hoped that he would enjoy the experience away with England!

We booked a week long package deal with a tour operator specialising in the region and flights were arranged with Bulgarian airlines, flying from East Midlands airport to Varna, on the Black Sea Coast. I even spent a few months trying to learn some Bulgarian as well. I bought a phrase book and spent most of my bus journeys to work trying to learn and remember some helpful words and phrases, such as "seven large beers please!" We also had to sort out an internal flight within Bulgaria, because the match itself would be played in Sofia, the capital, which is at the opposite end of the country from the resort in which we would be basing ourselves, Zlatni Piasaci, otherwise known as 'Golden Sands,' fortunately for us.

In order to make sure we obtained match tickets in advance, without the hassle we experienced in Toulouse, we decided it would be worth joining England Fans, the Football Association's name for their official supporters group. With England fans, we were pretty much guaranteed home tickets for Wembley games, along with having priority access to away tickets. I remember snapping up the tickets in advance and being pleasingly stunned when I found out the price: four quid. That's right, four quid for match tickets to a crucial European Championship Qualifying match. Most of the boys started to get the feeling that we would really enjoy this trip if those kinds of prices were typical of the country! My reading and research about the country seemed to back up that thought, as food and drink were ridiculously cheap from what I could gather. The internet was still in its infancy then, certainly in terms of mass public access, so most of what I managed to find out was from reading books like 'The Rough Guide to Bulgaria'. For this trip, instead of Coyney Tours sorting it out, the pressure was on me, as I'd volunteered to sort everything out in advance. Beckett Tours was up and running!

England had started the qualifying group in typically inconsistent form, going down 2–1 in Stockholm to a dominant Sweden, in a game which saw Paul Ince red-carded by the famous Italian referee, Pierluigi Collina. Kevin Keegan was at the helm nowadays after Glenn Hoddle was removed by the press, after making his ill-advised remarks about disabled people and faith healing. The FA bowed to the newspaper hacks, who forced him out. I went to one of England's better performances in the group, which was the 3–1 home victory over the Poles, at Wembley. Paul Scholes scored a hat-trick that day as England played the Poles off the park with a rampant attacking display. Luxembourg caused few problems, as expected, but then the Swedes came to London and forced a 0–0 stalemate, on the same day as our flight to Varna.

East Midlands airport suited us just fine, as it was just a short drive down the M1 from Sheffield. Packed in Ant's bag was the legendary 'Goldie' St George Cross flag, which had temporarily disappeared for a year or so, before being found again in our mate Kris' house. This England flag, which measured approximately 2.5 metres by 1 metre, was actually made for us by a couple of the lads' girlfriends a few years previously, so that my brother Oz and I could take it to Munich with us, during our trip to watch Forest. The legend 'Goldie', was stitched across the red cross in big, bold, black letters and refers to a local term of endearment often thrown about across our local pub, The Rag, as a type of greeting. "Ey up Goldie" Woody would say to you as you entered the pub, and the catchphrase stuck. It has since been alleged that the term 'Goldie' refers to someone having golden balls (as in, being lucky or successful with the opposite sex), but most of the lads are still in denial to this day as to whom the phrase was originally aimed at.

The three hour flight was great and we collected our belongings without difficulties from the carousel. We didn't have to look for a taxi as the tour company had buses waiting outside the airport, ready to take all their guests to different resorts along the coast. We boarded the bus heading up the coast to Zlatni Piasaci and decided that we should pop out for a night out as soon as got there, as it was just starting to go dark. It was a warm, balmy Saturday evening in Varna and many young people seemed to be on their way for a night out in the city centre. As our bus drove through the busy streets, I was struck by how many slim, pretty girls there were on the streets, seemingly all wearing tiny mini-skirts, which was fine be me! I suppose the stereotypical image of Bulgarian girls was more akin to large shot-putter types from the iron curtain years, but nothing could be further from the truth on this evidence, based on what I saw on that bus journey.

Our first night in Zlatni Piasaci, or Golden Sands, would prove to be extremely eventful and rather unfortunate. We were dropped off at our accomodation and I think we were all impressed by the standard of the hotel, which was a lovely four star place, right at the side of the beach. Perfect!

"Bleedin 'ell lads, we've landed on our feet here I think", remarked Scarecrow, as we scanned the hotel reception, which was large, spacious and full of marble. Attractive ladies stood idly by, not seemingly doing very much, almost as if they were waiting for somebody. We checked in and I changed some pounds into leva, which was the Bulgarian currency. I only changed about 100 quid, but the huge wad of notes I received back made me feel like a gangster, as it must have been about two inches thick. The local currency was very weak in comparison to strong currencies like the pound, but that could only be to our advantage on this trip. The cash struggled to fit in my pocket, so I reasonably assumed that I wouldn't be needing 100 quid for one night out here, so I left at least half of it locked up in my bag, in the room.

Once again, I ended up sharing a room with Deano, based on the fact that we'd coped fine in France as neither of us smoked, snored or had a tendency to emit foul odours from our backsides. We dragged the Goldie flag from Ant's bag next door and immediately tied it to our balcony railings, so that it could be clearly viewed from the main street below which separated our hotel from the beachside bar immediately opposite. Our room was on the second floor of five, the view was great and the rooms were spot on.

"Come on Beckett, get a move on," shouted Deano through the bathroom door, as I stuck some hair gel on. We walked down the stairs and found the rest of the lads waiting for us in reception, which was becoming busier.

"I reckon we try that beach bar over the road," said Jim. It looked very appealing, as it had a pool adjacent to the large bar and the seats were all of the padded, cushioned variety that makes you want to chill and relax in them for hours.

We headed down the hotel steps, across the little street and straight into the bar. I decided to practice some of my Bulgarian, which went down a treat, and a few minutes later, seven large beers appeared at our table.

"Cheers lads," said Met as we all clinked glasses and took in the sea view. This bar would become our 'local' for the trip and we ended up in there at least twice a day. We had another round before leaving, and when we got the bill we were over the moon (and you don't say that very often)! The beers had worked out at just 35p each! This was going to be some trip!

We went for a walk along the main promenade which ran parallel to the gloriously sandy beach. The sidewalks were full of cute little wooden shacks, which housed all manner of souvenirs that could satisfy anyone's taste, whether it be quality local food produce, retro clothing, kitsch and tacky mantelpiece type items or lots of Bulgarian wine. The prices were excellent and I resolved to make a few purchases to keep my girlfriend happy, later on during the week.

At 11.00pm, the street was still busy with people and very well lit. Most restaurants seemed to employ attractive young girls to stand outside their front entrances, trying their best to entice willing and hungry guests inside. We succumbed and went inside a pizza restaurant to fill our faces. A large pizza cost only around three quid, so again, we filled our boots with food and beer. It would be rude not to, at those prices. The local Zagorka beer had already become our beer of choice as it tasted quite nice and was available at a seemingly consistent price of between 30p to 35p, depending on which venue you entered.

Sat outside my favourite beach side bar in Bulgaria.

After leaving the pizza place, we sauntered towards the centre of the resort, which was full of bars and a few nightclubs. Then, we made an unfortunate decision, which ended up causing a horrendous couple of days for poor Jim. We walked into a lively looking bar, ordered some Zagorka, and then sat down around a large table, next to the open windows.

"What a top place this is," commented Scarecrow. "I'm going to try and get hold of some of this Zagorka stuff when we get back to blighty," he added.

"It'll cost you a fair bit more than 35p back in Sheffield, even if you can get hold of it," I ventured.

"Well, it beats Fosters any day," added Matt. "I'd sooner have me leg off than sup that shite." Fosters was a dodgy Australian beer that even they won't drink down under, so they sell it to us. It was readily available in many Sheffield pubs for some reason, presumably bulk price deals or moments of marketing genius.

Next to the table was an open wine rack and the bottles on it were not locked away behind a closed door. A few of us picked up a couple of bottles and had a look, trying to suss out the price, what kind of wine it was and where it came from. We then put most of the bottles back on the rack and sat back down. Just for a laugh, a few of the lads had taken a couple of the bottles back to our table, and as some of us were wearing those combat trousers with large side pockets, a few wine bottles got stuffed in them. After maybe twenty seconds or so, the wine bottles were returned back to the rack, with most of us chuckling along at the joke. All except for one, as Jim, engrossed in mid-conversation with Ant, forgot to take the bottle out of his side pocket. None of us really noticed this at the time, but it became all too apparent about ten minutes later.

We were talking about the upcoming match in Sofia, to be played in a few days, when we heard a screech of tyres outside. Two Lada police cars had pulled up next to the kerb and four policemen got out, rather calmly I thought, and walked into the bar. I wondered what they were up to and so I watched their progress as they moved through the busy bar. They were heading in our direction, but I thought nothing of it. Without warning, the first policeman got his truncheon out and pulled a shocked Scarecrow up from his seat, holding the truncheon around his neck to hammer home the point. Next in line was Matt, who was also dragged up from his seat with a rude, black truncheon around his neck. Met had been sat next to Matt on that side of the table, but he saw what was happening and stood up on his own voluntarily, which was probably a good move. We were all stunned, but decided to stand up of our volition, to avoid the truncheon. We stood there stunned, trying to protest with the policemen, but then they lunged towards Jim and grabbed him, before roughly pushing him towards the door. It was only then that we noticed the wine bottle stuffed into the side pocket of his combat trousers.

They moved quickly through the bar and marched Jim towards one of the police cars, whilst we tried to protest and argue with them. A large crowd had gathered by now to see what was going on, and for some reason, three of the policemen went back inside the bar, possibly to talk to the bar staff, and we were left standing around outside near the police car, whilst the remaining officer was putting handcuffs on Jim, who had already been bundled into the back seat. We looked around at each other.

"Quick, leg it!" said someone, and we all scattered in different directions, disappearing into the night. Matt, Ant and Deano went one way and I finished up running behind a hotel with Met and Scarecrow. We vaguely remembered the direction back to our hotel and so we stumbled towards it, steering clear of the main street and walking through darkness and dimly lit areas wherever possible, just in case the police were looking for us.

After about ten minutes, we made it back to our hotel and went in through the main entrance, scanning the street behind us. We all somehow congregated back in Ant's room.

"What the hell was all that about?" asked Matt, with an incredulous look etched across his face.

"God knows," replied Deano with an angry frown.

"I can't chuffin believe it," said Met. "We've only been in the bleedin country about six hours and one of us has already been arrested!"

"What a bunch of bastards," muttered Scarecrow, to which we all murmured our approval.

"Why did they go for Jim? Why him? What had he done?" asked Ant, searching for answers.

"He'd still got one of those wine bottles," confirmed Deano, with a resigned look on his face. "The bar staff must have phoned the coppers."

"Jesus, he wasn't going to nick it," I offered. "He'd probably just forgotten and left it there. Anyway, why didn't the bar staff come and talk to us?" I added.

"They were probably scared," suggested Matt. "Look, there are seven of us and England fans still have a bit of a reputation, don't they? They just took the easy option without confronting us. They'll have carted Jim off to the local lock-up now I reckon."

"Let's go down there now then and see what we can do," Scarecrow suggested.

"Don't be daft lad, there's nowt we can do now, and anyway, we don't even know where the nick is. We're better off asking our tour rep in the morning," Ant said in response.

I looked on my watch. It was 1.00am. Ant was probably right. After such a great start to the trip, this had to happen. Great. Just great.

We polished off another beer each whilst we sat glumly. We hoped to be able to find out what had happened to Jim in the morning.

We met downstairs for breakfast at around 9.00am and I think most of us were still looking over our shoulders, after what had happened the night before. The self-service food on offer at the buffet table consisted of grey scrambled eggs, grey poached eggs, boiled eggs, cheese, more cheese, some tough, hard bread and some kind of mystery meat salami slices, which all smelled a bit off. Ummm, what a selection.

After all choosing poached eggs on toast, we settled down to discuss a plan of action. Scarecrow and Met would talk to the tour rep and explain what had happened, whilst the rest of us were just to wait on the beach until Jim got back. I imagined Jim walking into the hotel at any moment, fully expecting him to rejoin us with his trademark chuckle and a cigarette.

I paid a few leva for beach chair hire and then I sat and talked to Matt, Deano and Ant on the beach whilst we waited for news, or Jim. A Russian couple nearby came up to us and warned us, in pigeon English, to apply lots of sun cream, as our whiter than white skin would get severely burnt in this sun. Typical. Even Russians were taking the piss out of our English sun-tans!

Scarecrow and Met turned up with sombre news. The rep was very supportive, but she said that Jim was being held at the police station, along with some other fans, and that they were considering pressing charges.

"Oh for god's sake, it's not as if he's stolen anything is it?" Ant countered, "as he hadn't even left the bar with it. How can they charge him for anything, when he hasn't done anything wrong?"

I think our suspicion was that the Bulgarian authorities were hoping to extort money from Jim or us, in order to secure his release, which was outrageous in my book. I still fully expected Jim to rejoin us at any moment. To be honest, I couldn't afford to chip in if we decided to bribe the police officers with a large amount of dough. Despite the cheap prices in Golden Sands, I was struggling to afford the trip. I was only getting paid fifteen grand in my job, back in Bristol, and I was struggling to clear some huge student debts. I also had a 'high maintenance' girlfriend at the time who was bleeding me dry. She didn't quite grasp the concept of paying for anything, or doing rounds, though she was happy for me to shell out of course, all the time.

In the event, it was actually the following day when they let Jim out. He was understandably pissed off. In fact, you could go so far as to say that he was extremely pissed off. He launched into a cigarette and beer frenzy as he felt that he had to make up for lost time on his holiday, and who could blame him? He said that he'd witnessed a Scouser getting beaten up in the jail by some rough coppers, simply because he'd been mouthing off constantly. Jim had therefore wisely decided to just keep quiet and not cause any problems, hopeful that he'd be let out shortly. All of us felt obliged to get the beers in for Jim that day, as he certainly deserved them! It could only be upwards from there for him.

Walking around Golden Sands, we continued to be mesmerised by the stunning women we saw around us, most of whom were happy to strut around in bikinis or very tight fitting, short dresses, whilst wearing high heels. Were they locals, or were they simply touting for business? Or both? Most of us had girlfriends at the time and we were all trying to behave, otherwise I'm sure we would have tried our best!

Later on the Monday evening we ventured into a bar that doubled as a strip club. Let's face it, we were seven blokes on holiday together, in a cheap resort, full of gorgeous women, so it was always going to happen, wasn't it? We paid a small fee to get inside and then we all gathered around one of the small stages, all of which had a mini catwalk leading up to it. It was waitress service, so we gladly received our seven large Zagorka beers and settled down to watch the show. The girls were simply stunning, mostly very pretty with slim, toned bodies. It was a tough job for us to be in there, but somebody had to do it! The girls would perform for about five minutes, then go for a break, with their place being taken by an equally stunning beauty almost immediately. The girls performed a strip tease, down to their tiny g-strings, before walking off and blowing kisses to the crowd. Their aim was to get as many tips as possible from the watching blokes. As we sat and gawped, our hands almost involuntarily went to our pockets and produced a wad of notes. You were supposed to get a few notes out and then politely position them somewhere around the vicinity of the ladies' g-string area, for which she would smile and pout even more at you. I think it's fair to say that most of us felt like James Bond in there, because we weren't used to having a thick wad of notes in our pockets, which we were more than able and willing to completely blow on glamorous women! The funny thing was that every time one of us gave a lady a wad of leva, we were safe in the knowledge that it was probably only worth a pound or two each time, which seemed like good value! Certainly better value than places like Spearmint Rhino at home, I would imagine!

As we scanned the room and chatted, we noticed quite a lot of tough looking blokes in black suits, who looked life mafia types to us. Some of them were simply standing and watching, whilst others sat at tables with two or three half-naked women draped all over them. We did venture the opinion that it could be a mafia owned place, so we all made sure not to pick up any wine bottles without asking first!

The next day we decided that Jim needed a treat, so a fishing trip was planned. We'd noticed a couple of blokes advertising half day fishing trips the other day, so we decided to take one of them up on their offer. The harbour was about a 20 minute walk, so being lazy, we decided to take advantage of the mini-train ride that shuttled along the sea front road. As luck would have it, there was a stop right outside the front door of our hotel, so it became too easy to hop on and hop off during the course of our stay, especially as the price for any trip was a matter of pence, not pounds. The train drivers all seemed to have long mullets for haircuts, so we presumed they must all have been Kajagoogoo fans. Either that, or they simply loved Chris Waddle's mullet in the early 90s.

The mini-train dropped us all off outside the small fishing harbour, where a couple of local blokes tried their best to make us choose their boat instead of the other one.

"I give you lunch, fresh fish, beautiful, lots of wine and don't forget, also salad," boasted one. He was an honest looking bloke and we liked his name, Yordan, which reminded us of a great Bulgarian footballer at the time, called Yordan Letchkov, who played for Hamburg in the Bundesliga. We gave him the thumbs up and jumped on board his vessel, which was called 'The Santa Maria'.

Scarecrow and Ant were feeling slightly rough, after putting away a few too many beers the night before, so they passed on the fishing part and just sat down, looking decidedly ropey. The movement of the boat on the waves of the Black Sea wasn't helping them one bit.

Yordan and Emil gave us a fishing rod each and then demonstrated the technique involved. I was totally clueless, as I'd never gone fishing before in my life. Needless to say, I caught absolutely nothing. Fortunately, they kept the supply of Zagorka coming along nicely, so I was never thirsty.

After an hour and a half of getting nowhere, the call came from Yordan.

"Come on boys, it's time to eat. We have fish!"

At this point, Scarecrow stood up and rushed over to the side of the boat and threw up overboard. There he was, doubled over, green shorts on, black T-shirt, green face. He had been looking ill for most of the trip, so we all hoped that would clean him out.

"Nice one Scarecrow," called Matt with a grin. Scarecrow didn't bother looking up, but he flashed two fingers in Matt's direction.

The lunch provided was average at best, but the local red wine was good. Yordan was a big football fan and he followed CSKA.

"2–1 Bulgaria," was his prediction for the big match tomorrow evening. "England no good any more, sorry".

We just laughed and came back with a few more predictions in our favour. With Alan Shearer in the team, goals were always possible. Yordan was very impressed that we were flying to Sofia early the next day, so he insisted on giving us a business card which belonged to his brother, who ran a local taxi firm.

"That'll come in handy," I said. "Blagodarya!"

Get the beers in lads! I'm sat having a coffee whilst Jim, Ant, Met, Matt,
Deano and Scarecrow down the beers.

Later on in the afternoon, we decided to have a go at archery and make a contest of it. A lady had a small tourist business operating close to our hotel and she had set up a few targets and was charging a small fee to have a go. The English have a fine history when it comes to producing skilled archers, which is something that goes back quite a few centuries, particularly during battles against the French. For this reason, we should have been inspired by our forefathers, but sadly, we were all useless. Personally speaking, I loved it, but our champion on the day was Ant, who somehow managed to get the highest total, despite wobbling somewhat from all the Zagorka and red wine he'd put away on the fishing trip. My time would come a few years later in archery, as I whipped my brother at Warwick Castle. I called myself Robin Hood for the rest of that day, whilst he became Friar Tuck!

We were just having a quiet beer in the hotel bar a little later on, when we were all incredibly shocked and embarrassed by one of our fellow countrymen. One of the tour reps was selling some match tickets at face value, as his company's head office in Sofia had supplied them. The majority of England fans who approached him departed gleefully, holding in their hands a golden ticket, for just four quid. Then a short, bald, skinny bloke covered in West Ham tattoos approached the rep and spoke in a broad cockney accent. He asked about the match ticket prices, to which our rep responded with a price in Bulgarian leva.

"Fackin ell, that's only four quid innit? These had better be legit, or I'm gonna come back and fackin smash yer kneecaps in! Alright?" With that, the moron departed. Even his walking style was aggressive.

We were sat nearby and heard every word. There was simply no need for it. The poor rep looked mortified, so Deano said "Just ignore him. He's just an idiot and probably didn't mean it". We just felt embarrassed to be honest. It's an awful thought to think that some cretins like that are in effect, ambassadors for their country when overseas. Sadly, a minority of people simply don't have the intelligence or respect for others that should be a pre-requisite for any foreign trip.

Matt and Deano enjoy the beach at Golden Sands.

Later on that evening we chose a different place to eat. It was a really nice bar with lots of outdoor seats and a guitarist strumming along to entertain the paying customers. The bloke on the guitar looked like my dad and played like my dad, though he had an undoubtedly Bulgarian accent, as opposed to my dad's broad Yorkshire dialect. He played a number of old 60s and 70s tracks familiar to most of the audience, who were mainly Western Europeans. He had a curious, but amusing habit of finishing each song with the words, "every time."

Matt loved to try and beat him to it, so when the guitarist had finished a Beatles classic, he jumped in first with a heavily accented "every time." The guitarist ignored him at first, but after he'd finished a rendition of '*Message in a bottle,*' Matt again shouted out "every time," in his best Bulgarian accent.

The guitarist smiled a weak smile and tried another number before his break, which was a dodgy attempt at Abba's '*Money, money, money,*' which left us all in stitches, especially when Matt belted out a loud "every time," to finish the set. We clapped the guitarist furiously as he carefully placed his guitar down and mopped his brow. Then, he came sauntering over to us, with a smile.

"Did you like my music boys?" he enquired.

"It was brilliant mate, very good," replied Met.

"Awesome mate. Have you got any cd's for sale?" joked Matt.

"Yes, you can buy them please," he replied. "I have some in a box next to my guitar if you like?"

"Get your money out Met," said Matt in Met's direction.

There followed a slightly uneasy pause for a few seconds, before the guitarist said, "I am Bago. What is your names?"

Matt then introduced all of us to him and he vigorously shook hands with the whole table. He turned out to be a good bloke who simply loved his music and he was very enthusiastic about practising his English with us.

"Matt sings in a band and plays guitar at home," I happened to mention.

"Oh really?" replied Bago. "That is fantastic. What kind of music you play?"

He wasn't too familiar with The Stone Roses or Joy Division, but he did ask Matt if he liked Queen, which elicited another laugh from the table.

"Is it alright if I have a go?" enquired Matt suddenly.

"What you mean, on the guitar?" replied Bago.

"Yeah, if you don't mind. I mean, I haven't played for a while, but I can show you some new songs if you like?" said Matt.

"Sure, that will be good," replied Bago. "Every time."

So it was that Matt finished off his Zagorka, then stood up and walked over to the microphone at the front of the bar, with the rest of us chanting his name and clapping wildly.

Matt played a few 'Enderby' classics, the names of which escape me, and of course we all shouted "every time" at the end of each of his songs. Bago was left nonplussed by Matt's lyrics and songs, but he definitely appreciated Matt giving him an extra break and the rest of the audience were politely supportive as well. You had to admire Matt for having the bottle and audacity to step up there, but then again I suppose he was used to it anyway. Sat up there on a high stool, strumming away, I couldn't take my eyes off Matt's black plimsolls, which were his trademark footwear of choice. We ripped him mercilessly for it, but he didn't seem to care and just laughed along with us, merely quoting the price to us.

"Seven quid lads, seven quid. You can't argue with that."

Matt plays to his audience in Bulgaria.

We left the bar and moved along the street, searching for a different drinking hole. We came to a larger, loud venue that sounded more like a night club, going on the decibel level inside. Met marched inside first, as it was his round. We stayed outside, as we were distracted by a poster advertising live music elsewhere. Suddenly, Met came storming back out of the club.

"Sod that lads, it's 50p for an ale in there!"

We cracked up laughing and took the piss out of Met as we slaughtered him, fairly I thought. It's funny how you can tune into the local prices when you're overseas and Met wasn't having any of it. To him, he was getting ripped off, as the standard price elsewhere had been no more than 35p! You had to laugh.

Met was insistent and he led us away, back onto the street. He wasn't going to pay 50p for a beer on his round!

We had a few more beers elsewhere at the far more reasonable price of 35p (!) and then went back to the hotel to try and get some sleep. We had to be awake at 5.00am in the morning, in order to get the taxis I'd booked to take us to Varna airport for the flight to Sofia. The big match was almost upon us.

Waking up with a hangover and a rough head is never nice is it? The sound of your alarm clock going off is similar to that of a pneumatic drill, in your mind, when it involves getting ready to go to work. Today was different though. I had an exciting reason to drag myself out of bed. A quick shower, a bit of hair wax, teeth done, deodorant spray on, all topped off with an England shirt and a pair of shorts. Oh, and my priceless match ticket, even though it only cost four quid!

Going to England or Forest home games usually involved a train ride, a car journey or a bus, but I'd never had to catch a flight on match day in order to arrive at the ground before. The taxis turned up and as we slowly worked our way out of Golden Sands, we noticed quite a few people still staggering back to their hotels at the tail end of a night out, just as the sun slowly started to rise.

The taxi driver had some loud music on, which certainly helped to wake us up. To my ears, it sounded like Turkish music, or certainly eastern influenced and high pitched, which is a style of music that doesn't agree with me at the best of times, never mind 6 o'clock in the morning. Bulgaria had been ruled and governed under the vicious grip of the Ottoman Turks for 500 years, before they gained independence in the late 1800s, so I suppose it was no surprise that the Turks had left their mark in a number of ways, one of which was the popularity and high pitched whine of middle-eastern music. Give me Blur or Oasis any day! The Bulgarians also enjoyed short, strong, black, Turkish style coffee and munching on sunflower seeds, as we would find out at the stadium.

The departure lounge at Varna airport was fairly quiet by the time we got there, though one or two businessmen started to come through from check-in with briefcases after a while. I hoped for their sake that this was not a regular commute. Imagine having to do that? Bulgaria was a fairly small country and the flight would last for little over an hour, but the cost must surely be prohibitive for the locals to do regularly.

A few Derby fans we'd met in a bar a couple of days earlier came through into the departure lounge and so we had a chat and a catch up with them. Despite following the sheep, they were good lads, if a little misguided. Their plan was the same as ours: fly to Sofia, spend the day looking around, go to the match, have a long night out afterwards, then catch the early 6.15am flight the next day back to Varna. It all seemed so easy and we fancied our chances of being able to stay awake in the early hours, even if it meant moving from bar to bar, or club to club.

When our flight was called, we hopped on the bus provided, which then drove us around to our waiting aircraft. We had a shock when we saw it. It looked like something out of an Indiana Jones film, with flimsy looking propellers on the front and wings, which helped to give it an early twentieth century look. In all honesty, it looked like it had been built shortly before the Second World War and we doubted whether it would actually get off the ground. It didn't particularly fill us with confidence, but we clambered aboard, took our seats and then spent ten minutes winding Ant up, who was a nervous flier, much like Dennis Bergkamp. If only Ant had the same ability on the pitch!

Surprisingly, the flight itself was fine. The plane didn't fly particularly high, so we had a great view of the Bulgarian countryside as we flew west, towards the capital. There was a handful of other England fans on the plane and we all acknowledged each other with a nod and a grin whenever someone stood up and walked to the toilet.

The police and airport officials greeted us with a collective stare and frown as we walked through the arrivals hall in Sofia, towards the bus stop. Every one of them must have been in some way related to Hristo Stoitchkov, as they all had a scowl etched onto their features, whether male or female, just like their country's star player. The police in particular did have an undeniably menacing appearance, dressed all in black, rather like Darth Vader, but without the helmet. They also each had a truncheon and a pistol, both of which slotted into a holder on a belt.

"Have you seen that?" commented Met. "Make sure you behave Jim," he joked. Jim replied with a simple two-fingered salute.

"Come on goldies, over here," I said, heading in the direction of a yellow, single-decker bus. I had studied enough Bulgarian to know what the City Centre was in cyrillic script, so after observing the sign above the driver's window, we all got on and headed towards the back. We had no bags with us, so no-one would have guessed that we'd just flown in to the city. The tell-tale signs that we might not be locals were the England shirts some of us were wearing. The bus tickets were ridiculously cheap, as expected, and we settled down to enjoy the ride.

The outskirts of the city didn't look particularly glamorous, as pretty much all we saw were ugly tower blocks, side by side with more ugly tower blocks. Many of the pavements were in a state of disrepair and neglect, and there were minimal road markings on the main roads, as well as poorly maintained, overgrown grass along the side of the streets. It did look like a country struggling to leave the communist era behind. Most of the cars being driven were ancient looking Ladas, or the infamous East German Trabants, which were the iconic Eastern European vehicle of the 70s and 80s, at least to us in the relative prosperity of the west.

Many of the tower block walls were plastered full of graffiti, some of which was vaguely football related. 'Levski boys rule!' screamed one large, blue slogan. 'CSKA red boys,' offered another, unsurprisingly scrawled in bright, red paint. Levski and CSKA were the two biggest clubs in the city and indeed the whole country, certainly in terms of crowds, star players and trophies won throughout their respective histories. CSKA were the team who had knocked my beloved Forest out of the European Cup in season 1980–81, and the big match later that night was to be played in their (rather small) stadium, over the other side of the Borisova Gradina Park in the city centre. Levski had larger crowds and played in a bigger stadium, but sadly it was closed for refurbishments back then in 1999, so the match had to be moved to the smaller venue.

As befitted the tradition throughout much of communist, Eastern Europe, Levski were sponsored and financed by the much feared Secret Police, whereas CSKA received the backing of the army. In practice, this meant that both teams were often on the receiving end of fortunate refereeing decisions, certainly in the domestic league. Most of the country's better players were also 'encouraged' to join these two clubs, either through bribery or state sponsored threats. Subsequently, both the secret police and the army divisions of government received regular, timely, propaganda boosts whenever the two sides won, which was very often.

The state backing of the two clubs didn't stop problems whenever the two sides actually played each other though. The 1985 Bulgarian Cup Final between the two clubs featured two dubious penalties, two red cards, a handled goal (much like Maradona's infamous 'goal' in 1986), a series of scuffles and a push and shove fest like no other, during which the referee was struck twice by Levski's goalkeeper, Bobby Mihailov. After the final whistle, a full-on brawl broke out between the players, including a young 19-year-old Hristo Stoitchkov, who didn't hold back in his duties for CSKA, who actually won the match 2–1, though it seems irrelevant compared to the other events that marred the day. As a punishment, both clubs were actually dissolved and those players involved in the worst of the violence received lifetime bans, including Stoitchkov. Political pressure ensured that these punishments were later reduced and revoked, ensuring the survival of the two clubs and Stoitchkov's presence at the 1994 World Cup, as well as a glittering career overseas with Barcelona.

We got off the bus at what looked like a lively looking square, full of cafes and shops. We had no particular plan, other than to explore the city all day and slowly make our way towards the stadium in time for the evening kick-off. As we walked across the street, Met narrowly avoided being run over by a speeding tram, though the tram lines in the street should have given him a clue about potential dangers in the area.

I did have a copy of my 'Rough Guide to Bulgaria' book shoved into my pocket, but none of us were the museum or church types, so we were content to let fate decide the day's events.

So of course, we found ourselves outside a bar, by pure coincidence. Once again, the waitresses left us staggered by their beauty, but we'd become used to that over the course of the week. We soaked up the sun and the Zagorkas and reflected on how much better this was in comparison to Toulouse the year before, mainly because we could relax, safe in the knowledge that we had the precious match tickets. We were taking it in turns to carry the Goldie flag, so I displayed it across the backs of our chairs, so that it could be easily viewed from the busy main road that ran past the bar. We hoped to somehow get the 'Goldie' St George Cross flag to be shown on live television later on, but that rather depended on how easy it would be to get down to the wall or the running track around the edge of the pitch. We were motivated by the thought of friends and family watching back at home, or in The Rag at Stocksbridge. We could all picture Woody in The Rag, stood up and pointing at the screen, shouting in a broad Yorkshire accent: "Ey up Goldies!"

We left after about an hour or so and Scarecrow said, "look, we'd better do something touristy, cos my mum will want to know what I've seen, apart from the football and the inside of pubs."

"You've been in a McDonald's as well, don't forget. What more could you want?" I laughed.

We headed towards the Church of St George for a quick look, partly because of the name, but also because it was supposed to be the oldest building in Sofia, with parts of it dating from the 3rd century. To be fair, it did look extremely old, but most of it had been rebuilt anyway, after numerous occupations and conquests over the centuries. It was a fairly small red and brown brick building which looked out of place in its much more modern surroundings. We had a quick look before Met piped up again.

"Come on, the pub's open!"

As we walked along the boulevards and avenues of the city, we couldn't help noticing the large number of military statues taking pride of place in several squares and alongside busy thoroughfares. Most of them were large, dark and undeniably militaristic, in the classic communist style, with figures raising weapons or tools to the sky in almost celebratory style. A huge amount of graffiti now surrounded all the statues we saw, which was presumably the work of disenchanted youth, angry at the lack of jobs, money and opportunities, as the country struggled to leave the communist era behind and fully embrace the free market conditions prevalent in most of Europe. At the time of our visit in 1999, corruption and mistrust were endemic throughout many aspects of Bulgarian life and it was also one of the poorest states in the whole of Europe, with poverty and unemployment levels much higher than the European average.

After amusing ourselves at some funny shop names, such as 'Smeg,' we then headed towards the Alexsander Nevski church, in the square of the same name, because it was probably the most noticeable landmark in the whole city, which was a place with few landmarks. It was also vaguely in the direction of the stadium and we were now in the middle of the afternoon, so heading that way made sense. It was a genuinely impressive building, but what surprised me was the fact that it was really a memorial to dead Russian soldiers who'd lost their lives fighting for independence for the Bulgarians, from the Turks, during the Russian-Turkish war in 1877–78. We didn't bother going inside, but the large white building with a huge golden dome on top was certainly worth a look and a photo opportunity.

We then crossed Alexsander Nevski Place, which is a huge open space, towards a large statue of a lion that Jim had spotted. It was another photo opportunity for us, so we all clambered on top of it and had a few pictures taken with us all grinning and holding up our England flag for all to see.

It was at this moment that we were approached by the one and only Nick Collins, the *Sky Sports News* reporter. He'd obviously seen us larking about and thought we'd be likely candidates for a television interview! I'd last seen him on Sky Sports about a fortnight earlier, reporting live from outside Old Trafford about a Man Utd story, but it was nice to meet him in the flesh, so to speak. We chatted about Sofia as a city, and he wasn't a fan of the place, possibly because he'd been to so many lively, beautiful cities over the years and Sofia didn't really compare with the likes of Paris, Barcelona, Rome and Athens. His trademark moustache was very impressive, I have to say, and he was polite and professional in his request to interview us. Scarecrow feigned shyness, but eventually relented and lined up in front of the lion statue for the cameraman. Nick then moved along the line, one by one, along with his sound man, asking us for our thoughts and predictions about the big game.

Scarecrow was first up. "Ummmm, er, it'll be 2–1 England tonight I reckon," he mumbled.

"I'm confident that it'll be 3–0 to England," commented Jim.

Nick and the sound man then came to me, so I offered my thoughts. "I think we'll get a 2–0 away win tonight, with Shearer and Sheringham getting the goals."

Nick then changed his tack when it came to Matt. "What do you think of Sofia?" he asked.

This threw Matt a little bit, as he must have had a good line prepared about the score, so he came up with "not a lot!" to which we all smirked.

"2–0" said Deano.

"1–0 England," offered Ant.

"3–0 or 3–1 to England," suggested Met.

To this day, I've got no idea whether or not the interview was broadcast on Sky Sports, but I'd like to think that our collective good looks and charm offensive might have won the editorial team over! My only other possible television appearance came a few years later in 2005 at Newcastle train station, when a Tyne-Tees television reporter interviewed me on the platform just after I'd got off the train from London, shortly before the England v Azerbaijan game to be played that day. They were after a line about how disappointing it was that Newcastle wouldn't be hosting any more England games after the Azerbaijan clash because the new Wembley stadium was almost ready to be re-opened. I think I delivered a good line that day, so maybe I made it onto the Tyne-Tees news bulletin!

We headed off in the direction of the Bulgarian Army stadium, venue for the match a little later on. As we walked down the Boulevard Vasil Levski, we were accosted by a very friendly bunch of Bulgarian fans who insisted on taking some group photos of us. We were more than happy to go along with it, so we presented our best poses and grins as we held aloft the Goldie flag and more than a few Bulgarian flags. Various other local fans on their way to the game also came over to take photographs of the English fans and again, we obliged.

In Sofia, 1999. Nick Collins, of Sky Sports News fame interviewed us immediately after this picture was taken.

As we posed for what seemed like the twentieth picture in a row, I got a nasty shock. I received a swift, hard smack on my right cheek. I'd just been punched from behind. I was stunned more than anything, but the blow did hurt. I looked around to see a young lad sprinting away from me at a fast speed. He looked no older than about eighteen from my view, but he was already a good fifteen metres away. I was about to give chase when I noticed three nearby policemen staring at me, with hands on their truncheons. They must have observed me being hit, yet they did nothing to chase the culprit. In a split-second, I rapidly decided not to bother giving chase, as those Bulgarian coppers only had eyes for me. We'd already had one lad locked up and I didn't fancy being the second. I was also desperate to see the match. Common sense told me to just take it on the chin, so to speak, and move on. I could just imagine the policemen grabbing me as opposed to the halfwit who'd decided to ruin a good moment.

The rest of the lads didn't even see it. They were busy smiling for a camera, as we'd all been, and at first they thought I was winding them up.

"It must have been one of those Levski boys," smirked Ant, referring to the earlier graffiti we'd noticed. I was not amused.

Our path to the army stadium took us through the Borisova Gradina Park, past the Levski stadium, which was being refitted and refurbished, which was a shame as it was a much bigger venue. As it was, the second choice Bulgarian Army Stadium was an 18,000 sell out and boy, did we have a shock when we saw it.

After negotiating the police cordon surrounding the stadium, we entered through the turnstiles and saw in front of us, a grass bank. No concourse, full of bars and food outlets, but a grass banking.

"Gordon Bennett," uttered Ant. "Is this a footie ground or are we back at Bracken Moor? (He was referring to a series of football fields back in Stocksbridge, which were separated by grass banks on a slope.) Unbelievable!"

I was desperate for the toilet, so I looked around the gravel at the bottom of the grass bank, without success. My only option appeared to be to climb the grass bank, which I did on account of my bladder, which was fit to burst after all that Zagorka. After climbing for about fifteen metres or so, I came across a shabby looking tent, about six metres across and three metres wide, which, on closer inspection, turned out to be the toilet! There were four holes dug in the ground, with a little partition in between each 'amenity'. I didn't notice any sinks, any running water, any soap, mirrors or anything that you would expect. Nothing! It was like a badly constructed tent at the Glastonbury music festival, though the toilets there are better! It was incredible to think that this was supposed to be a UEFA approved stadium, fit to host a vital European Championship qualifier between two international teams!

It also goes without saying that it stank. I was lucky that I didn't need a number two, because all my grunts and groans would have been easily audible to anyone in the vicinity and I would have had only a flimsy piece of tarpaulin to pull across the entrance to preserve my modesty! How the women and children would get along with it I have no idea. It really was scandalous when you think about it. It made me wonder if it was only the away fans who had to suffer with this facility, or whether the home fans actually had recognisable amenities to use or not? I never got to find out, but at least the rest of the stadium looked slightly better than our away end, once we'd located our seats. Yes, real, actual, red, plastic seats.

The seven of us were sat on the same row together, which was six rows from the back of the uncovered stand. The view of the pitch was decent enough, apart from the fact that an athletics track separated us from the field, which is a fairly standard thing across continental Europe, unfortunately. The whole stadium was surrounded by trees in the adjacent park, which towered above the much smaller stadium. The only objects taller than the trees were the floodlights. The whole stadium was uncovered, apart from a small section of the main stand, which was presumably where all the officials, journalists, television commentators and bigwigs sat.

For me personally, it was still a great moment. For the first time, I was actually inside a stadium, ready for an England away game! I tried to soak up the atmosphere and savour the moment, so I got my camera out and snapped away. As kick-off approached, the crowd slowly grew until the whole place was packed to the rafters. The Bulgarian fans were incredibly noisy, despite the small size of the crowd. As is common throughout Eastern Europe, their fans blew long and hard on a little wind instrument called a zurna, which sounded like a kazoo to me, and was rather like a duck quacking! The sound given off was a weird, bizarre whine, to English ears, and I would go so far as to say that they sounded even more annoying than Scottish bagpipes, which is saying something. The Bulgarian fans also had a large number of flags on show, as their patriotic feelings were made clear for everyone to see.

Met and I walked down to the edge of the track and tied up the Goldie flag, hoping that it would be viewed on television. The police officers who ringed the pitch just stared at us blankly, without expression. It reminded me of my trip to watch Forest play away in Munich against Bayern, in 1996. There, the police officers and stewards actually took the flags from our fans and neatly laid them out for us on the running track. At the end of that game (we lost 2–1) the stewards actually folded up the flags and politely returned them to us. I was very impressed, I have to say. I couldn't imagine that happening at any English ground, to be fair.

The scoreboard behind us read Bulgariya 0 Anglia 0 in cyrillic script, which is hard to decipher. If the goals started to flow I'm sure we would have figured it out! We really needed to win this one, if we hoped to qualify for the finals, which were due to take place the following year in Belgium and Holland. England's record in the European Championships was moderate at best, as all we'd ever managed were two semi-final appearances, in both 1968 and much more familiarly, in 1996. We'd already dropped more than enough points in this qualifying campaign, so we could do without conceding further ground to the Swedes, who were looking good at the top of the table. Bulgaria had already been to Wembley and achieved a creditable 0–0 draw, as they sat back and frustrated an England team who couldn't find a cutting edge on that day.

It was also a major game for the Bulgarians, because although they couldn't realistically make the finals, it was Hristo Stoitchkov's final game for his country. He'd announced that he would be retiring some weeks earlier and he'd chosen this game, at the very end of the season, to call it quits. To them, Stoitchkov was like a cross between Bobby Charlton, Geoff Hurst and Gary Lineker, all rolled into one.

The teams came out to a crescendo of noise and we belted out the national anthem, even though I believe 'God Save the Queen' is the wrong anthem for England. GSTQ is a British anthem and not an English tune. The Scottish and Welsh have their own anthem for example, so why should the English have to put up with a British anthem, instead of an English classic? In my opinion, we should have 'Jerusalem' or possibly 'Land of Hope and Glory' as our national anthem, or even Baddiel and Skinner's 'Three lions!'

Bulgaria 1 England 1, in 1999.

The England team that day featured a young Jonathan Woodgate at the back, who was making his debut. Up front, we looked strong, with Alan Shearer, Teddy Sheringham and Robbie Fowler all promising goals, though as the match progressed, we looked a little unbalanced to me. The manager, Kevin Keegan, had been suffering from criticism in the press about his lack of tactical awareness and indeed he eventually resigned just over a year later, admitting that the job was beyond him.

After 15 minutes the away end exploded in celebration. Michael Gray swung in a high ball from the left, which was knocked back to Alan Shearer, who turned and struck a low shot into the corner of the net from about 12 yards. 1–0! We went berserk and I have a very distinct memory of jumping on Scarecrow in celebration: I think I almost broke his neck!

Sadly, a fragile looking England defence conceded only three minutes later. Stoitchkov whipped in a free-kick from the right hand side, which was headed in by Georgi Markov, who looked unmarked. The locals went ballistic, whereas we frowned, swore and muttered. I was also surprised that he'd recovered from his supposed murder by poisoned umbrella tip some decades previously! I can only presume that it was a common name in that neck of the woods.

At half-time, some Levski boys to our left started throwing firecrackers and smoke bombs onto the pitch and there was even a short 'handbags' fight between five or six of their own morons. The police, unlike our own, stormed right into the middle of it and started whacking anyone within striking distance with their truncheons, in an indiscriminate manner. They then dragged away a few teenage lads and marched them towards the tunnel, before they disappeared out of sight. I really hoped that the muppet who had clouted me was amongst them! After seeing and hearing stories about how the police acted over here, I was glad that I wasn't in their shoes.

About fifteen minutes from the end of the game, the police down on the running track started wading into our end, by walking across the tops of the plastic seats to form a solid line of standing, raised officers which split the English support into different sections, for some reason. I was sat down, with a police officer standing on the chair next to me, hand on his truncheon, staring at the fans around him. To say that it was an intimidating action would be an understatement. The fans who were actually sitting on those seats were just told to move out of the way! I really couldn't see any need for it at all, as the behaviour of the English support had been exemplary. The long line of officers stretched from the back row all the way down to the running track and they were positioned no more than three or four seats apart. Fortunately, nothing happened, but it again left me puzzling over some foreign policing methods, which could only be viewed as confrontational.

After lots of huffing and puffing from both teams throughout the second half, the match eventually ended in a 1–1 stalemate. It was a reasonable result in a tricky away game, but we still felt that it was two points dropped. We were kept in the stadium for a good thirty minutes or so at the end and a significant number of England fans chanted and pointed in the direction of Kevin Keegan, who was hiding in the dressing room: "You don't know what you're doing. You don't know what you're doing!"

As we exited the ground, Ant was particularly nervous.

"I'm shitting meself," he admitted, when I asked him. "Jim's been locked up, you've been smacked and did you see the way those coppers whacked their own fans in there? I'm watching me back," he added.

All the England fans seemed to be heading in the same direction, which was back through the park towards the city centre. I wasn't sure who Ant was most scared by: was it the local fans or the local police? Anyway, he soon started whistling the theme tune to *The Great Escape*, which was already a popular tune amongst most England fans. Sure enough, within a few seconds, hundreds of England fans were whistling along as we walked in almost total darkness back through the park, which didn't seem to have any lights switched on. If a large group of local nutters were going to try and jump us, the conditions were perfect for it.

Fortunately, we had no problems and we made it back to the main roads and light! We were all feeling a bit peckish, so we stopped at a fast food place and grabbed a dodgy kebab or three. We walked a bit more, looking for a decent bar, but we ended up getting lost. We spotted a chunky looking policeman sat astride a motorbike, so Met decided to ask for directions. Luckily, this one was friendly and he was only too happy to point us in the right direction, using our map.

We ended up in the Sheraton Hotel bar, which was affordable for us, if not the majority of the locals. It was a very smart, swanky bar, the kind of bar that had a white piano in the corner and waitress service, with a bow tie for staff being de rigeur. Just like The Rag in Sheffield then! We settled on an outside table and took full advantage of the waitress service as we relaxed and reflected on the game. After a couple of hours, you couldn't see the top of the table as it was almost completely covered in Zagorka bottles, as they obviously weren't too bothered about clearing tables in that place.

We finished up in another bar for a while, but by that time, we were all drained and exhausted after our early start and long day. We decided to hail a taxi and head back to the airport, even though we still had a few hours to kill in the early morning. The thought was that we might somehow manage an hour or two of sleep in the airport lounge. The taxi driver already had a copy of the morning's newspaper, which was full of photographs from the match. "I'm very sorry, very sorry," he kept repeating, as in his mind the draw was not really what England needed in order to qualify.

When we reached the airport, it was practically closed. Nothing was open and could we find any spare seats to sit down or sleep on? Of course we couldn't. Ant decided to wrap himself in the Goldie flag and then curl up in a heap on the floor!

We eventually got the flight back to Varna and tried (and failed) to get some sleep during the short journey. Most of the rest of the day was a write-off, as we slept and snoozed through the heat, missing out on a day's sunbathing and ogling on the beach.

Ant curled up inside the St George Cross flag in Sofia Airport.

During the late afternoon, we went up to the hotel's rooftop bar, which afforded a beautiful view of Golden Sands. There we were, shirts off, factor 30 sun cream plastered on, enjoying another Zagorka or two, when Ant came and joined us, and then showed off possibly the reddest, maddest mosquito bite I'd ever seen. He reckoned he must have been bitten in Sofia the day before, whilst walking through the park. Despite that, he was still happy to test out another Zagorka beer and we all admitted that we'd dropped lucky here, with a cracking hotel and a great bar. One or two of the glamorous ladies ever present at the bar, or downstairs in the reception hallway, were giving out 'business' cards and openly touting for business. The hotel staff didn't seem to mind, possibly because they received some commission from the ladies, or maybe because it was perfectly normal and acceptable behaviour to them. Either way, none of the staff ever seemed to bat an eyelid when one of the prostitutes acquired a customer. We did hear a story about a German tourist who had his passport stolen during one business encounter in his room, so I hope it was worth it for him!

Later that evening we went out for a meal to celebrate a great and eventful holiday. The restaurant was in a beautiful setting right by the beach, and as the sun set, the scene was undeniably romantic. I looked across the table opposite me and saw, instead of a glamorous girlfriend, the faces of Met and Scarecrow. What a let down!

We spent some time studying the menu, which was varied and impressive.

"What are you having?" Matt asked his big brother.

"Pizza," replied Ant.

"Ummm, I'm going for pizza too," said Scarecrow.

"What are you nailing?" said Ant in my direction.

"To be honest, I do fancy that Meat Feast pizza mate!"

"Sod it. I may as well have pizza as well then," added Jim with a grin.

Met and Deano also plumped for a pizza, which just left Matt. He pretended to thoroughly scan the menu and discussed the merits of the lobster option, or the foie gras, but with a chuckle, he eventually succumbed after ensuring that he had a captive audience. "Meat Feast pizza it is then!"

When the waiter came we struggled to get our order in as we were laughing too much. We must have sounded like a right bunch of dipsticks when Matt requested "seven Meat Feast pizzas please!" How sophisticated!

It reminded me of a different lads trip to Berlin, which featured some of the same crew, with a few minor additions in Paul, Oz and Boro Graham. Scarecrow had spent months beforehand practising his German language skills before the trip and even showed me his phrasebook. He studied and studied and impressed us with one or two phrases on a Friday night in The Rag. When it came to the actual trip however, he was reluctant to speak any of the native lingo. We were in Berlin for three days and I hadn't heard him speak a single word of German. On the final day, we were in a restaurant just a couple of hours before our departure flight, and in a similar fashion to the Bulgaria trip, we all ordered tomato soup as a starter. The waiter looked disapprovingly at us as Paul put in the order.

"Seven tomato soups please."

When we'd finished, the waiter returned to our table and asked us how the food was. Without a stumble, Scarecrow instantly replied, "Wunderbar!"

We fell about laughing, with tears creeping down our faces, and we struggled to speak for a minute or so. It was Scarecrow's only German word during the entire trip. Maybe you had to be there.

After we'd finished the meal, we managed to get ourselves split up, as Matt, Ant and Jim went off to a bar which the rest of us couldn't find. After ten minutes of searching, we gave up and went into a cool, air-conditioned bar. In the days before regular mobile phone use it wasn't always that easy to meet up with people at the same time!

I sat on a tall stool next to the bar, alongside Met, Deano and Scarecrow. I'd read about a Bulgarian spirit I fancied trying, which was called Mastika, so I ordered one. It was an anise flavoured drink very similar to Greek ouzo, which I loved. I always had a bottle of Ouzo 12 at home after discovering it during several previous trips to Greece. Anyway, the drink came with ice and a tiny bit of water, again just like ouzo, and I thought it tasted just great. I managed to persuade the other lads to try one and they went with it, maybe because it was a nice change to Zagorka and red wine.

Three German lads joined us at the bar and we all got talking, partly about football, but also about Bulgaria, women, drink and the like (but not penalty kicks). Klaus, Jurgen and Lothar were good lads and spoke pretty good English, so we ended up getting on well. I've no idea if they were their real names, but they were each given famous footballer's names by us and our witty Sheffield minds. Before long, we were all buying each other rounds of Mastika, which continued to taste absolutely delicious to me, whilst costing next to nothing.

After a couple of hours drinking we eventually stood up and I felt absolutely fine. We bid farewell to our German friends and headed towards the electric doors, which willingly opened for us.

As the fresh air hit me, my legs suddenly felt unusually heavy, and after a few more steps, they just gave way and I collapsed in a heap on the ground. For some reason, Deano, Met and Scarecrow thought I was just messing around. Either that, or they were also too drunk to see where they were going or recognise their surroundings, so they just carried on walking, in an apparently aimless direction. The problem was that I could not physically stand up. My legs had completely packed up and my head was spinning. I'd felt absolutely fine in the bar, but the Mastika was really kicking in now and I tried hard to think about how much I'd drunk. The other lads had given up on the Mastika after a while and returned to an old favourite, Zagorka beer. How I wished I'd done the same!

As I couldn't stand up, I had little option in my drunken state than to roll. My mind was alert enough to want to avoid being picked up by the Bulgarian police force in one of their black Lada cars, so I rolled beside a parked Trabant at the side of the road, making sure that I was on the beach side of the car so that I wasn't visible from the street.

I must have fallen asleep for a while, because when I came round the sun was slowly rising in the sky and the German tourists were already heading for the beach or the pool with their towels. I tried to stand and this time, fortunately, I succeeded. I stumbled back to the hotel, which was about a ten minute walk away, and I entered the hotel reception just as a large group of tourists were heading out in the opposite direction, wearing swimming trunks and bikinis, with towels slung across their shoulders. Yes, I was late coming in! Or early, depending on how you want to look at it.

We flew back later that same day and I decided that I needed to give my liver a rest for a while. I certainly didn't visit the local off-licence looking for a bottle of Mastika!

As it happened, England did eventually manage to qualify for the Euro 2000 finals after beating Scotland in the play-offs. A Paul Scholes double in Glasgow ultimately did the damage to the jocks. Once there though, England flattered to deceive once again. After racing into a 2–0 lead against Portugal, we managed to claw defeat from the jaws of victory and went down 2–3.

The following game against Germany was better, as we beat our rivals in a competitive game for the first time in ages, thanks to an Alan Shearer header. I watched that game in Soho with a bunch of friends from Sheffield, Boro Graham and some kiwi girls, who happened to be my flatmates at the time. I think the whole event passed them by somewhat, but we were happy to educate them about the round ball game, as being kiwis, they were rugby fans.

We needed just a point against Romania in the final group game to qualify for the quarter-finals. With the score at 2–2 going into the final minute, we were looking good, but then Phil Neville had a brain explosion and tripped the Romanian winger in the box when he was going nowhere. It really was a schoolboy error. The penalty was despatched and we lost 2–3 again. That last minute penalty knocked us out of the tournament, when we should have had a quarter-final to look forward to.

I was living in London at that time, and as I walked home disconsolately from the pub, I almost gave an old lady a heart attack as I walked behind her, as I suddenly screamed out "Bloody Phil Neville!" in disgust and frustration, perhaps no more than a metre behind the old dear. Being a passionate England fan certainly causes moments of grief, anguish and despair.

Chapter Three

PORTUGAL 2004

A lot of things had changed by 2004. I was living in Twickenham and working as a teacher. I'd also managed to get myself married the previous year to an Assyrian girl from Iraq who has Australian citizenship, so I ended up getting married in Sydney. I still made sure that Maureen was very much aware of the exploits of Wayne Rooney and the rest of the England football team, and fortunately for me, she is a football fan, which meant avoiding a lot of unfortunate pain that some people with football loathing spouses have to go through.

News of our exploits in Bulgaria and France had travelled around The Rag pub in Stocksbridge over a couple of years and lots of people wanted to try out the Beckett Tours experience. I'd had the European Championship finals on my radar for quite a while, as I thought that Portugal, in June, would again be ideal for a trip.

I'd gone up to Sunderland in April 2003 with Met, Paul and Scarecrow to see England smash Turkey 2–0 in a qualifying match. England played really well and attacked throughout the game, until goals from Vassell and Beckham assured a much-deserved victory. Wayne Rooney in particular was excellent throughout the match, as he constantly teased and tormented the Turkish defence, with his dribbling runs scaring them. The atmosphere was tremendous that night, easily one of the best, loudest and most partisan England home crowds I'd ever been a part of.

We'd been in a pub earlier in the day, just standing around having a chat, when a local bloke asked us where we were from.

"Sheffield," I replied.

"Huh, just as I thought," he said. "Bloody southerners!"

It is to date, the one and only time I've ever been called a southerner! I suppose that to a Mackem in Sunderland, most people were southerners, apart from Geordies up the road in Newcastle.

In October of that year, England had to go to Turkey and face a hostile, intimidating crowd in Istanbul, but we came away with a 0–0 draw that saw us qualify for the finals in Portugal, despite David Beckham blazing a penalty high over the crossbar. I watched the match with Paul, Five Bellies and my brother Oz in a pub in Twickenham, and once the result was obtained we had a huge celebration for the rest of the night, as it meant that our planned trip to Portugal the following summer could now go ahead!

The number of willing travellers for Portugal 2004 was much larger this time and some of the lads found it easier to get a free pass for the trip from their girlfriends if they invited them along as well, as they sold it along the lines of a nice, romantic summer holiday! To be fair, I also wanted my foreign missus to experience the magic of an England abroad trip, and we thought that the Euro Finals in Portugal were ideal. For work reasons, we could only manage a week, but that was still better than staying at home and missing out.

The draw for the finals took place in December of 2003 and England were grouped with France, Switzerland and Croatia. We decided that we'd go out for the Croatia match and get as many tickets as we possibly could, through whatever sources. The game was to be played at the famous Stadium of Light in Lisbon, which suited us as our first choice base for the trip was Lisbon, as opposed to other host venues like Porto or Coimbra. I booked those of us based down south on a British Airways flight from Heathrow, whereas those based up north arranged flights from Manchester.

My brother Oz and his girlfriend Katie were coming with us for their first England trip abroad. They both lived in Kent and worked in the pub trade, as they'd run several pubs over the years in places like Canterbury, Ightham and Wadhurst. Katie was a token Arsenal fan, but our Oz had spent years trying to convert her to Forest, with little success it has to be said.

Also coming along to Lisbon were Kris and his South-African girlfriend Cathy. Kris used to be my next door neighbour in Sheffield, but he had moved down to London a few years previously, where he'd met Cathy. They lived together in Wimbledon, where Kris tried to keep alive his passion for Sheffield Wednesday, which can't have been easy.

Matt was bringing his girlfriend Lyndsay along to Lisbon, after promising her a romantic week in the Mediterranean. I didn't have the heart to point out that Lisbon faced the Atlantic, as opposed to the Med.

Met was back for more shenanigans as well, though this time, like me, he was also bringing his wife, who was called Bev.

Sheffield United supporting Paul had also decided to grace us with his presence on this trip, presumably because he wanted to sample a better quality of football than that served up at his beloved Bramall Lane. His girlfriend Sue, a Blackburn Rovers fan, was also coming along.

Jim was the only singleton on the trip and therefore the only one who didn't need to be responsible!

As the finals approached, I still hadn't decided how I would manage to get time off work. As a teacher, it's not easy to get time off during term time, as our holidays are good enough as they are. I wasn't sure whether to ask for unpaid leave (and make up a convincing reason for it, like I was to be best man at someone's wedding overseas), or whether I should just go sick. It was easy enough for everyone else, as they'd just booked time off from work in the usual way, months in advance.

England's team at the time again gave us cause for hope. Sven-Goran Eriksson's players had qualified without excessive concern, and with players like Wayne Rooney, David Beckham, Paul Scholes, Steven Gerrard and Micheal Owen in the team, the England fans again hoped that this time it might actually happen. Most of these players had taken part in recent huge successes like the 5–1 away win in Germany and the 1–0 World Cup win over Argentina, so optimism was the general mood of the day.

As the tournament started, I still hadn't decided how to blag the time off work, which I know was leaving it a bit late. As luck would have it, I was presented with the perfect excuse for taking time off, though the circumstances themselves were extremely unfortunate for me personally. I blame that bloody Zinedine Zidane.

For England's opening match against France, I'd gone to an unfamiliar pub in Twickenham, in order to watch the game. I'd gone along with my brother Oz, as well as Maureen, Katie and four visiting girls from Australia, who'd all come to see my wife in her new surroundings. I'd spent a good ten minutes telling them how good the atmosphere in the pub was going to be, even if they didn't know anything about 'soccer,' as they called it.

Sure enough, the pub was full to the brim, despite the fact that we were very much in rugby territory, as Twickenham rugby stadium was only a ten minute walk away. England played really well and took the game to the French, and a powerful Frank Lampard header opened the scoring for us. In the second half, we were awarded a penalty when Rooney was tripped by French keeper Fabian Bathez, and Oz and I gleefully punched the air as we all waited for the formality of Beckham putting us 2–0 up from the spot. Except that he didn't. His miss seemed to invite the French to attack us more and we dropped far too deeply for my liking. With two minutes to go, we were still 1–0 up and I imagined that all the customers in the pub collectively had their fingers crossed.

Then, the nightmare started. Careless errors by both Gerrard and Heskey gave away a penalty and a free-kick, both of which Zidane converted in little over two minutes. When the referee blew the final whistle, we were all devastated and deeply shocked. How could we have snatched defeat from the jaws of victory yet again? We were 1–0 up with a few minutes left to play and victory was ours for the taking, but then two individual errors gave the game away in unbelievable circumstances. It was an absolute calamity.

Most people in the pub seemed shell-shocked and I struggled to speak for a minute or two. Some people left the pub, but most stayed in and Oz and I decided to get one more round of drinks in at the bar. When I turned around with a few drinks in my hands and moved towards my wife, I noticed that a couple of young lads were talking to her. I asked her to come and get her drink, so she moved towards me and took her glass. I was just starting a conversation with her when I was suddenly jumped from behind, as several punches rained down on my head. I tried to protect my wife from any blows, but by the time I'd turned around the culprits had sprinted out of the pub. My brother had taken a few blows to the head as well and was just getting up off the floor. All the poor girls we were with were stunned, angry and shocked. The bouncers on the door were nowhere to be seen and a large space had opened up around us. A few people asked us if we were alright, but I think we were just stunned and in a state of shock for a few minutes, before any kind of pain kicked in.

The unprovoked attack probably only lasted 10 or 15 seconds or so and we were left seething with rage at the unjustness of it. What kind of animals choose to attack a couple of blokes and four girls for no reason at all? I guessed that there might have been four of them, but I didn't really get a chance to look as it all happened so quickly, and I was focused on protecting my wife's head and for some bizarre reason, trying not to spill the drinks I was holding! The bar staff were clueless and useless and we were left to sort ourselves out due to the disappearance of the bouncers.

My jaw and cheekbone were hurting a bit so I went to the bathroom for a look in the mirror. I couldn't see any blood, or any marks to be honest, but there was a mild pain in my right cheekbone.

We walked back to our flat seething with anger and frustration. I also felt embarrassed that our guests from Australia had witnessed such a shocking incident. We resolved to report the incident to the police, as well as having my cheekbone checked out with an x-ray.

At the hospital, the doctor confirmed my suspicions: my cheekbone had been fractured in two places. I was told by the specialist that I needed to have two, small, metal plates inserted into my cheekbone to hold it together, and that these would have to be screwed into the bone. I would obviously need to go under anaesthetic and my cheekbone would ache for a while, but the specialist assured me that any pain would ease over the course of a few weeks until it ceased, in theory of course. The operation was scheduled for twelve days time, which meant I'd be out in Lisbon for most of that period, before coming back and visiting Hammersmith Hospital for the necessary surgery.

As you can imagine, I'd had better days. I found out later from a friend of mine called Dave that the pub where the incident took place was renowned for punch-ups and fights, which were mainly caused by morons coming into Twickenham from the less desirable parts of Feltham and Hounslow, which were just a few miles away. He'd know, because he's a local policeman. Sadly for me, I was unaware of this when we entered the pub, so I just had to put it down to experience. We were all just in the wrong place, at the wrong time, and I was unlucky.

As a little side note to this, I imagined that once the metal plates were inserted into my cheekbone that airport security scanners would always beep for the rest of my life, every single time I passed through them. Fortunately, it never happened, presumably because the plates were so small. After the operation had taken place, I have to say that I was amazed by the skill and precision of the surgeons involved in fixing up my cheekbone. They shaved part of my hair above the right ear and then made an incision there. Another cut was made inside the top right hand corner of my mouth, and somehow, using two metal rods, they were able to put the screws in place so that the tiny plates would hold the bone together. Both the incisions were stitched up by the time I awoke to see their handiwork. I was really impressed, I have to say. I ended up shaving my hair all over anyway, because I thought the shaved part near my ear just looked ridiculous, so I thought I might as well go the whole way and I plumped for the number two look.

The fortunate side of this story is that I suddenly had a great excuse for getting time off work! The doctors had signed me off for a month, which absolutely suited me, what with a European Championships taking place and every game being showed live on television. There was also the small matter of the upcoming trip to Lisbon and having a very real excuse for not going in to work was a big weight off my shoulders. Not that I would recommend anyone having to go through what I went through!

I developed some dark bruising towards the top of my cheekbone, just underneath my eye socket, so from a distance it could have been mistaken for a black eye. I didn't want to present the image of someone who gets involved in punch ups (even though I had!), so as we lined up at the check-in queue at Heathrow, I did feel rather self-conscious. Maureen (or 'Mo') tried to cheer me up, as she could probably tell that I felt a bit uncomfortable, what with the dull pain and the 'shiner'.

"Look, if anyone asks, you can just say that it's a football injury. You could say that someone had accidently elbowed you as you both jumped for a header," she suggested. I liked the idea, so I did!

Our Oz and Kate were also in the slow moving queue and we were all still grumbling together about the unjust and unfortunate incident in Twickenham a few days earlier. The excitement of a trip to Lisbon was just about taking over though. We'd got the guide books and so the girls in particular were looking forward to visiting a number of tourist must-sees, as well as enjoying the football atmosphere.

"I'd really like to go and see the castle," offered Kate. She loved her history and was fascinated by castles and other ancient buildings, as were a few of us.

"I'm more interested in trying to get into the Stadium of Light for the match to be honest," chuckled Oz. My brother, along with all the girls, didn't have a match ticket, as the game was sold out and he wasn't prepared to pay the ridiculous prices that most ebay sellers were asking for. The rest of us had got our tickets from the Football Association, with the exception of Kris, who'd actually bought his ticket from an ebay seller in Hong Kong. We'd been taking the piss out of him for weeks, firstly in predicting the non-show of his ticket, and then secondly, when it did actually arrive, in insisting that it must be a dodgy forgery and that he'd get turned away at the gate on match day.

The queue for the British Airways flight was extremely long and extremely slow, but we eventually managed to check in on time, just, and clambered on board for the short two hour flight. We mostly discussed the previous evening's game, which we'd watched at home for understandable reasons. England had got themselves back on track with a solid 3–0 victory over a decent Switzerland side in Coimbra and all the talk was of Wayne Rooney, who had another impressive game. He was direct, skilful, physical, positive and confident and at that time, he was still somewhat of an unknown to many European defences. He'd bagged a brace against the Swiss, to go with his impressive performance against the French, and he was fast becoming our main hope, despite his tender years in 2004.

When we arrived in Lisbon, we made our way through the terminal to the bus stops, as we didn't want to get ripped off by any taxi drivers. It seems to be an unwritten rule around the world that taxis picking up at airports will always rip you off and charge extra for bags and suitcases, and if you're a foreigner who can't speak much of the language, you're even more prone to having your wallet emptied. I'd sussed out which bus to catch and where to get off as I'd been reading up at home. The others were flying in from Manchester on later flights and were staying in different hotels to us anyway.

Lisbon looked an attractive but very old city at first glance, and we kept looking at road signs and checking where we were on the map I'd brought with us as the bus trundled along. As we came to the Marques de Pombal statue and the roundabout encircling it, we got off and walked up the Rua Braancamp to look for our hotel. I'd booked it back in December, but prices were already stratospheric back then, as Lisbon hoteliers rubbed their collective hands together in glee and looked forward to ripping off all the foreign tourists expected for the finals.

I'd settled on a basic looking three star establishment, simply because the better looking hotels were asking for a laughable amount of money per night. It looked unspectacular from the outside, but we didn't really expect much anyway. We checked in as quickly as we could, dumped our bags in the basic rooms and then headed off out for a lunchtime stroll.

We walked back down to the Marques de Pombal roundabout, because that was where the nearest metro station was. My guide book mentioned that the roundabout itself was renowned for being Lisbon's worst traffic headache, especially at rush hour, and it was easy to see why. It reminded me of the Arc de Triomphe roundabout in Paris, as several lanes of cars criss-crossed in chaotic style without crashing into each other. The flags of the sixteen competing nations were nicely spread out around the edge of the road and huge, gigantic posters of the Portuguese team were draped across balconies and windows surrounding the square. There was definitely something going on in this town!

We got the metro down towards Praca Dom Pedro IV, which was a large square known colloquially as 'Rossio,' which also happened to be the name of the metro station. I was shocked to see a blind man without legs playing the accordion and begging on the steps as we climbed up into the sunshine. It was our first sighting of the poverty and desperation that did exist in this city, despite the government's obvious attempts at smartening up the place for the finals. Mo gave him a few coins, as she was always prone to doing.

As we walked into the square, it was impossible to miss the thousands of small Portuguese flags that hung from windows or plant pots on verandas, as they were simply everywhere. Rui Costa, the Portuguese star player, seemed to have his face plastered on every bus shelter advertisement as well. You could say that the locals were definitely up for the tournament, unlike our experience in the south-west of France in 1998.

The Portuguese had a bad start though, going down 2–1 to Greece as the expectations and pressure got the better of them. They had a huge game coming up here in Lisbon in just a few days time, against their ancient historical enemy, Spain. It was a game they really had to win to progress through to the quarter-finals. England were in a similar boat, needing to beat Croatia to get through to the last eight, because of the shocking ending to the France game.

We strolled down through the streets of Baixa towards the waterfront, where we'd arranged to meet the rest of the lads (and girls!) later on. For some strange reason, I bought a silly Portuguese bandana 'hat,' which resembled something Sascha Baron Cohen would have worn when acting as his infamous 'Ali G' character on television.

We had an hour or so to kill before we met up with everyone else, so Mo and Kate were more than happy to browse around the shops, whilst Oz and I trudged behind them in protest. We slowly coaxed the girls down towards the Praca do Comercio, which was another large square at the side of the River Tagus. We found a likely looking bar facing a huge, beautiful arch called the Arco Triunfal and settled down for a drink. I sent a text message to Met and Paul to let them know where we were.

We'd only been in the city for a short while, but we were impressed by the architecture all around us, the huge squares, the imposing statues, and the fact that the city was blatantly, completely in party mode, which was a feeling we would see confirmed when the Portuguese played the Spanish a few days later.

The first beer of choice for Oz, Kate and I was Sagres, a popular Portuguese brand. We always believed in sampling the local delicacies! Mo was a very light drinker at the best of times, but at least that made her a very cheap date! She was more than happy with a Coke or a cup of tea, which didn't exactly fit the image of the typical football fan.

"Alright Goldies," muttered a familiar voice. We turned around to see Paul grinning, along with the rest of the Manchester flight crew.

"Ah, nice of you to join us," I replied. "Welcome to Lisbon."

"It looks quite nice," offered Bev.

"Yeah, I'm quite impressed with what I've seen so far," I replied.

Handshakes and hugs followed, along with the odd peck on the cheek. Not for the boys you understand!

"That Rossio place is buzzing," said Kris. "It looks like the place to be lad!"

"Let's just sit down and enjoy the view for now," smiled Lyndsay, as she pushed Matt towards a vacant seat.

"What's the plan then Beckett?" asked Met, happy to leave the tour guide role to somebody else.

"Whatever you want it to be Goldie," I replied. "Let's just suss out the place and squeeze in a few drinks wherever we can," I added.

"What you supping?" asked Jim.

"Sagres. It's alright," I replied. "Nine euros though."

"Nine?" asked an incredulous Kris.

"That's cos we're sat in the middle of a blatant tourist spot," Oz responded. "If you're on about drinking, we'll be far better off if we get away from all the main squares, otherwise we'll run out of cash."

"Good call lad," agreed Met. "Get the first round in then Jim," he added, to which everyone chuckled.

Kate, Lyndsay, Cathy, Bev, Sue and Mo soon gathered around Kate's guide book to look up museums, shops and castles, whilst the rest of us talked football and beer. It was a great spot to be in, and as a few of us had England shirts on, we received a few thumbs up every now and again from passing fans, or even the occasional shout of "In-ger-land," which is the time honoured way to greet fellow fans in pastures new.

"Which game is on tonight?" asked Kris.

"Italy v Sweden," replied our Oz.

"Where do you fancy watching it then?" asked Paul.

"Not this pub," said Met. "Not at nine euros for an ale." Bev gave him a friendly slap and smiled.

After a couple of drinks and some food we walked back up towards Rossio, through the Baixa district, which looked reasonably modern now in places, even though at one time, it was one of the oldest areas in the city. Much of it was destroyed during the 1755 earthquake, an event which inspired a massive rebuilding programme, led by the Marques de Pombal, known by some as a dictator who didn't like to take no for an answer. He must have been liked by someone, as he had a statue in his name close to our hotel.

As we walked along at a leisurely pace, a group of Spanish fans spotted my brother and started pointing and chanting at him.

"Rooney! Rooney! Rooney! Rooney!"

I found it hysterical of course, despite the fact that our Oz bore little resemblance to England's main striker, other than the fact that he had very little hair and was slightly chunky in stature. Oh, and the fact that he was wearing a red England shirt. Some unkind people have also said that our Oz looks like Shrek, the cartoon character, and our Wayne was also plagued by similar accusations.

We wandered around for a bit and then decided to go back to our respective hotels, get showered and changed, ready to meet up later for the Italy v Sweden match.

"Meet back here at the statue," said Jim. "7.00?"

Later that evening, we found a nice looking restaurant with lovely outdoor tables, near to Rossio Square. The waiter initially looked perplexed when we asked for "a table for thirteen please," but he was eventually able to accommodate us, crucially, within sight of the TV screen.

The Italians and the Swedes played out a 1–1 draw, which we

half-watched, to be honest. It was such a stunning, warm evening and we were all in holiday mode, enjoying the banter, the beer and the beauty of the square. This particular restaurant also served snails, which I had tried before in France, so I challenged everyone to order some and have a go. The only ones to take me up on the offer were Oz and Matt, with Paul in particular turning up his nose. Paul was the kind of bloke who was happy with familiar, non-adventurous food, so whenever he went overseas he tended to stick to McDonald's or KFC wherever possible. There was no way he was going to attempt snails, as that was just a bridge too far for his stomach!

"No chance," was his abrupt reply to my suggestion. "There's more chance of Met getting a round in," he added.

The snails were served in a garlic sauce and came delivered in their shells. They taste a bit like mushrooms in my opinion, and when covered in a garlic sauce they really are very tasty.

"You must be mad," shouted Paul from across the table. "I'm sticking with garlic bread!"

I managed to get myself in a bit of a row with a stuck-up waiter as well. He brought the wine menu over to our side of the table and then returned to ask us what we wanted. I hadn't been looking at it to be honest, as I was busy chatting away, so I said, "I don't mind. I'll have a bottle of any house red," as I looked over at Oz.

The waiter pulled a face and said, "That is not a good attitude. Wine is to be savoured and appreciated I think."

I wasn't best pleased with his attitude to be honest, as I had only been hinting at the fact that somebody else could choose the wine. Our Oz fancies himself as a bit of a wine aficionado, so I was giving him a chance to jump in and choose something for us. Anyway, put it this way: he didn't get a tip from me, the smarmy git!

Later on, I decided to try a local speciality called a 'caipirinha' in a bar. To be honest, the drink actually originates in Brazil, but there were so many Brazilians here in Portugal, their former colonial rulers, that it had become ubiquitous in the bars around Lisbon. After coming a cropper at the hands of the powerful Mastika in Bulgaria, I was a bit apprehensive at trying another unfamiliar drink, but this one was alright and didn't give me any nasty side effects a few hours later! Its main ingredients are cachaca (a spirit made from sugarcane juice), limes and brown sugar and it goes down well on a summer's evening. Not that I planned on trying to order one back in The Rag! I think the most sophisticated drink they served in The Rag was probably a pint of Castlemaine XXXX!

Just a couple of minutes walk away from the restaurant was the Elevador de Bica funicular ride, which went straight up the hill towards the Bairro Alto, a rabbit warren of ancient, cobbled streets. It also happened to be an area full of small, quirky bars, which appealed greatly to us. The tiny, cramped funicular was good fun to ride and it was definitely worth the two euro fee to get up to the top of the steep hill from Rua de Sao Paulo (yet another nod to Portugal's historical links with Brazil).

The journey up the hill only lasted a couple of minutes and it certainly wasn't fast, but once at the top we were afforded a stunning view of the centre of Lisbon, so we snapped away and took loads of tourist-style photos, as you do. We then set off enthusiastically along the narrow streets to look for a friendly looking bar. We came to a crossroads in a cobbled, traffic-free area and noticed a mini-bar and a fridge up against a wall, where a young bloke was serving cans and bottles of Sagres to passing customers. We asked how much the beers were and he responded with a smile etched across his face. "For you, it is only one euro my friend."

As you can imagine, we were all eager to pay for this round, so we all dug deep into our pockets! This particular spot became a regular haunt for us on this trip, as we were all used to standing in packed pubs at home anyway and didn't mind the fact that there were no chairs around. All of us that is except for my wife, who wasn't exactly a big drinker and she wasn't too keen on standing up! She was usually far happier sitting down in a bar and staying there, especially if it was winter time and a gale was blowing outside. Fortunately, I managed to sweet talk her with the offer of an ice-cold coke on this lovely, warm evening.

Lisbon 2004, with a much bigger group!

We stayed there for a while until a couple of the ladies needed to use the toilet, of which there weren't any, so we moved on to a graffiti covered bar that was playing chilled out Brazilian music. We'd had enough beer by this time to feel braver than usual, so a few of us got up on the tiny dance floor to show our non-existent moves. Oz asked the DJ if he had any Smashing Pumpkins, to which he responded with a blank, vacant expression and a shrug of the shoulders.

It was a top night and a great introduction to the city. We managed to somehow hail a few taxis and we all sped off back to our respective hotels in the early hours, feeling absolutely knackered but happy.

The next morning we all met up at the side of the River Tagus, as we'd all decided to go and visit the 'Jesus statue' over on the other side of the wide expanse of water. Surprisingly, there wasn't too much in the way of facilities or attractions down by the river's edge, but there was a regular ferry service over to the other side of the water, which we all jumped on for the short journey. There was a road bridge across the water a bit further along called the Ponte 25 de Abril, but we didn't have a hire car and it looked too far to walk down to. Anyway, a little boat ride appealed more to the ladies, so that was that.

Once on the other side of the river we set off exploring yet more ancient looking, cobbled streets. The houses there were looking the worse for wear and most of the tiny balcony railings we saw were all covered with rust, as presumably, the owners or tenants couldn't afford to protect or replace them. Despite this, almost every house or apartment had a little Portuguese flag hanging from a window or a plant pot, much like the rest of the city.

We staggered up the hill in the heat towards the statue of Christo Rei (Christ the King), which stands impressively, looking down on the river and the Ponte 25 de Abril (which was named after the 1974 revolution). The statue itself is a smaller version of the famous Christ the Redeemer statue in Rio de Janeiro, but it still looked impressive in scale to us as we glanced up at it, squinting through the harsh sunlight. The sensation of looking down over the bridge was a little weird, but fantastic. It reminded me of Golden Gate Bridge in San Francisco, both in shape and scale.

After taking a number of obligatory photographs, we marched back down the hill and I grabbed a much needed coffee before we caught the first ferry back over the Tagus. We headed back up to the bustling square known as Praca Dom Pedro to find it absolutely rammed with Spanish fans in high spirits. It was match day in Lisbon and the hosts were facing their ancient, historical rivals in a must win game. As the Portuguese had lost their opening game, surprisingly, to the Greeks, they simply had to win to progress through to the quarter-finals, whereas the Spanish would go through with a draw. As their team had less to do later on, it probably helped to explain why the Spanish fans were looking relaxed and in holiday mode. Most of their flags included a black silhouette of a large bull which featured prominently. Everywhere we looked we were met with a wall of red and yellow. The atmosphere was friendly and good-natured, even though the odd local driver would drive past with arm extended out of the window, single digit raised, in the vague direction of anyone who looked Spanish.

We spent most of the rest of the day enjoying the pre-match atmosphere and just walking around, taking in the sights. The occasional beer was forced down our throats of course and even my missus had one, which was a rarity.

Met and Mo meet a friendly Croatian.

We decided to watch the game in a restaurant, provided we could find one that had a decent sized television for us to ogle. We met up in the Biarro Alto, at the top of the funicular ride, and once everyone had arrived from their respective hotels, we wandered off in search of a likely looking venue that would be happy to host 13 English football fans.

It didn't take long. We spotted a cosy looking family restaurant and ventured inside, primarily because the only signs outside were all in Portuguese, and Met and Paul had a theory that we were less likely to get ripped off if we avoided the tourist traps. We looked at the prices and recognised a few of the dishes, so we were all in agreement that this looked an excellent choice, especially as the prices were so cheap! To our dismay, that all changed once the proprietor discovered that we were English. He picked up all the menus and disappeared into the kitchen, returning a few seconds later with a whole heap of menus written in English. That would have been thoughtful of him, if it wasn't for the fact that the prices were suddenly well over double what they had been on the locals menu!

"Are you having a laugh?" asked our Oz, with a blatantly disdainful expression on his face.

"Sorry boys, and ladies," he stammered. "This is the menu for the tourists."

"But we want the menus we looked at first," I protested. "We're not paying these prices," I added, pointing at the tourist offering in front of us.

The bloke wouldn't budge, so we uttered a few insults and departed in disgust. The fool had passed up the opportunity of making money from thirteen hungry foreign tourists, most of whom also enjoyed the odd drink or six. He could have made a fortune from us, but decided to commit commercial suicide instead.

We managed to find another place about ten minutes later, where the menus were written in Portuguese, Spanish, English and German. Paul was happy because they offered chicken and chips! More importantly, they had two large televisions up in the main dining room, so the blokes all tried to sit at the long table facing the screens, in order to get a good view of the match. Once Mo and Kate realised our strategic plan they slapped Oz and I with a smirk, which we happily accepted.

The prices were reasonable and they seemed happy to have us. We were treated as a bit of a curiosity in all honesty, as you could tell they hadn't received many English guests before. The local fish was delicious and the service was pretty good really, taking into account the fact that the Portugal v Spain game was now in full flow. We certainly got stuck into the 'vino tinto' and enjoyed sampling a variety of local reds, as well as more than a few glasses of Sagres. The staff looked over the moon to be making such a killing, and when Portugal scored a late winner the place erupted.

We left and headed towards our new favourite bar, which was the bloke selling cheap beer for one euro from his mini-fridge, at the edge of the street. As we stood and chatted, the area slowly filled up with elated Portuguese fans, waving flags and banners and blowing on air horns. More and more of them filed past, singing, dancing, waving and jumping into fountains! It was party time in Lisbon!

For the locals, beating their ancient, local rivals was one thing, but going through to the quarter-finals of their home tournament was another thing entirely. They were absolutely loving it and we joined in and sang a few songs with them, once we'd picked up enough of the words. Jim, Met, Matt and Lyndsay joined in with a conga dance, which was funny enough, but then Met decided to go mental with a large Portuguese flag that he had 'acquired.' Looking rather like a crazed caricature of 'Bez' from The Happy Mondays, he frantically waved the flag around his head in every direction imaginable, despite the fact that the flag was at least as big as a four-wheel drive vehicle. That's what beer and red wine does to you children!

We also spotted a fair number of Spanish fans walking past, most of whom looked disconsolate, but there were still some who were up for a laugh and a good time. We traded songs with a group of eight Spanish lads, which was rather amusing. We had no idea what they were singing, apart from the obvious "Espana, Espana," but we offered them some of our best lines, including classics like, "You're so shit it's unbelievable!" and of course, the time old, "In-ger-land, In-ger-land, In-ger-land" which eventually saw them off!

Bev and Met were a bit the worse for wear, so they grabbed a taxi shortly afterwards and headed off for some much needed rest and recuperation. The rest of us ploughed on admirably, well aware that we would probably have to do all this again the next night, as it was the day of the big England v Croatia game.

As luck would have it, we bumped into a group of four Croatian lads, all wearing their traditional red and white chessboard shirts. Oz greeted them with a beautiful rendition of "Who are ya? Who are ya?" with a finger jabbing in their direction. Fortunately, they seemed amiable enough and were happy to stop for a bit of banter about the game. I suppose it also helped that there were a lot more of us than them! They made some vague predictions about a Croatian victory, or some such nonsense, to which we just humoured them with laughs and bad jokes. We'd certainly see a lot more Croatians the next day.

It had been another brilliant night in Lisbon and I was absolutely loving the place by this time, despite some of the tourist rip-offs, which were an expected annoyance I suppose.

We all met up for breakfast the next morning at a cafe which happened to be conveniently situated near to our hotel, which saved us a tube ride. Most of us had our red England away shirts on, which was the pre-arranged uniform for match day. We knew we'd all be out for the day, so why not get your match gear on early?

The excitement was definitely building as we reminded ourselves that today's match was the main reason for our trip. We noticed England fans everywhere, filling seats at cafe tables in almost every street we walked through. When we eventually entered Rossio Square around midday, we were taken aback in amazement. The scene was astonishing. The whole square was covered in St George Cross flags, no matter which way you looked. Small flags, huge flags and medium sized flags, most of which had the home town or preferred football team of its owners plastered all over them. Huddersfield, Plymouth Argyle, Everton, Ipswich Town, Bournemouth, Bristol Rovers, Southampton, Leeds, Darlington, Truro, Manchester City, Worthing, Birmingham City, you name it. Oz and I spotted a Forest 'A-block' flag, so of course we rushed over and posed beside it, having thrust the camera in Mo's direction.

It was an impressive spectacle, without a shadow of a doubt. The

England fans had attached flags to poles, lampposts or fences, as well as draping them over statues, so that no-one could possibly be in any doubt as to which team was in town that day. I'd thought that the colour and the spectacle of the Spanish fans the day before had been a brilliant sight, but this was stepping it up a notch or three. Curious locals walked or drove by, but there wasn't a hint of animosity to be found anywhere, just the universal appreciation of football on a big match day.

It was barely past one o'clock by the time we'd finished walking around and soaking up the atmosphere in the square, so we decided to head up to the castle to do some more sightseeing whilst appeasing the ladies, as we were in no doubt that there would be the odd souvenir shop or six up there, and Lyndsay and Kate's fingers were just itching to get into their purses.

Oz, Paul, Katie and Mo get into the spirit. Probably too many spirits by the look of our Oz.

The Castelo de Sao Jorge sits majestically at the top of a hill, overlooking Rossio Square and much of the downtown city area. The view really is stunning from up there and it was definitely worth the walk. Some people who will remain nameless actually caught a taxi up the hill, despite it being no more than a ten minute walk. Mind you, it was 27 degrees on that day, so I suppose energy needed to be saved for the raising of celebratory glasses later on!

Exploring the castle and its surrounding grounds was a good way to spend an hour or two. It had been rebuilt and added to on several occasions over the centuries, but that didn't detract from a good stroll. They'd even left a couple of cannons overlooking the city to remind us of the castle's original purpose.

Most of the ladies left happy as well, as purchases ranging from fridge magnets to handbags were made at several of the tourist shops up there. Then Met started to get itchy feet.

"Come on, bloody 'ell, it's beer o'clock. The pub's open!"

We accidentally found ourselves sat outside a bar within a few minutes stroll, and the beer drinking began in earnest. Some of it was down to sheer excitement and some of it was down to nerves, as we were all aware of how important this game was. Then again, it could just have been down to the fact that most English lads like beer!

We cruised around a handful of bars in and around Rossio Square for a fair few hours, before deciding that we needed something to line our stomachs. We found a restaurant with a huge, long table that sat all of us comfortably outside. It was there that we saw our first Croatians of the day, surprisingly, as the whole city centre seemed to be swarming with England fans. Media reports from England were suggesting that there was between 60,000 to 70,000 England fans in Lisbon for the match, and having been there I can say that was definitely plausible. There was no way that all English fans had match tickets though, much like my brother and the girls, who had missed out through not being members of the England Fans club. They could possibly have got hold of tickets through a tout, but none of them were prepared to pay the 500 euros asking price, which was ridiculous.

Kris had dropped lucky when his match tickets did actually arrive from the Hong Kong based ebay seller, whereas the rest of us had just gone down the official route and got tickets priced at face value through the FA.

We arranged to meet Oz and the girls back at a bar in Rossio Square after the game, as they seemed content to find a decent venue to watch the game in. I was proud of Mo, because despite being a proud Aussie, she still had a red England top on, happily supporting her adopted team and having a whale of a time, despite not really being a drinker. Wasn't Oz lucky, going to the bar whilst being surrounded by all those ladies?

The rest of us departed and got on the metro at Restauradores, heading north-west towards Benfica's famous Estadio da Luz stadium, which translates as The Stadium of Light. Sunderland fans, I'm sorry to have to tell you that your stadium on Wearside is not the original version. At one time, this Stadium of Light had the largest capacity of any football ground in Europe, at a staggering 120,000 people, but even now, after redevelopment for Euro 2004, it was still capable of packing in over 65,000 punters.

As we approached the stadium itself we had to get through a couple of security checkpoints to make sure that we had tickets and that we weren't hiding any weapons. It is a hassle, but sadly necessary on occasions, if it's done properly.

We made it inside and climbed up many flights of stairs and several ramps, until we finally made it to our seats. We couldn't complain. We were near one of the corners, high up in the third tier, but the view was superb nonetheless. The stadium, when empty, bears a slight resemblance to the new Wembley, or possibly The Emirates at Arsenal. Mainly because the seats are all red and there are similarities in the stadium design and structure.

Met went off to try and acquire some beer, whilst I sat down and tried to take it all in. As the stadium slowed filled up, it was hard not to notice the proliferation of England flags, which seemed to cover every part of the ground, aside from a small corner in the lower tier, over on the other side of the stadium, which was the section for the Croats. They were heavily and hopelessly outnumbered by the English when it came to making noise and singing, so we just hoped that the same would be true on the pitch.

The sound was deafening when the players finally came out onto the pitch and into a white-hot atmosphere. Both teams knew that it was a case of 'winner takes all' and you would hope that the England players were buoyed by the sight of thousands and thousands of their fellow countrymen and women, over here to support them on foreign soil. I would conservatively estimate that there were at least 45,000 England fans present that night in the ground, if not more, along with many others, such as my brother, watching the game in a nearby bar. The level of support England receive is completely disproportionate to the level of success we achieve on the field, so I suppose that is purely to the credit of the supporters, who are nowadays easily the best and most loyal supporters in the world, in my opinion.

It was nice to see 'red' Gary Neville and 'scouse' Steven Gerrard with arms around each other's shoulders during the national anthem, which hinted at some form of unity within the squad, as most fans have heard rumours about Manchester United and Liverpool players not necessarily getting on like a house on fire when on England duty. Hopefully, it will remain just that: unsubstantiated rumours. To my mind, playing for your country has to rise above anything else, including club rivalries, so hopefully the vast majority of the players also think along similar lines. I know the clubs pay their wages, but representing your nation, your country, should remain the absolute pinnacle for a player, even in these insane times of silly salaries in the Premier League era.

Paul was busy videoing the fans singing 'God save the Queen,' but I'm not a fan of this anthem. To me, that is a British anthem and doesn't really represent England. The Scottish and Welsh don't play the British anthem, so why should we? They play their own national tunes, as they should, so England must also have its own. Maybe the choice of new national anthem could be put to the vote?

The famous Italian referee, Pierluigi Collina, was the referee for the game, which I was more than happy about. Generally speaking, he had tended to be a lucky omen for England down the years, with us grabbing a few wins during important games that he had officiated in. He's not the best looking bloke in the world, but those piercing eyes and the intense glare he projects seemed to help him gain respect from most coaches and players across Europe. He also reminded me of one of my favourite singers, an Australian front man called Peter Garrett, who used to sing in a band called Midnight Oil. He had an amazing presence and stature, helped by the fact that he was also completely bald and almost seven feet tall. Incredibly, Garrett is now heavily involved in Australian politics and sits in their Parliament House.

The game kicked off and we all tried to settle down and enjoy the match, if 'enjoy' is the right word. I was too tense and excited to be honest, so I spent most of the time sat on the very edge of my seat.

Disaster struck in just the fifth minute of the game, when a free-kick was swung over from the left and Kovac tapped in from just a few yards, after a bizarre deflection off Ashley Cole's knee had forced a reflex save from David James, which he could only push out towards the onrushing Croat.

Surprisingly, it didn't particularly dishearten me, as England had started the game reasonably well and it was so early that there was still all the time in the world for England to recover and come back, and so it proved.

Croatia v England in Lisbon's Stadium of Light.

In the 40th minute, England got back on level terms with a Paul Scholes header, which sent us all ballistic. Ashley Cole had the ball on the left hand side and he swept it inside, towards Gerrard, who played a wonderful first-time ball through to Lampard. Frank took a touch before putting Michael Owen through on goal, but Butina, their keeper, came out quickly to smother the danger. Unfortunately for him, the ball looped up in the air to Wayne Rooney, who intelligently headed the ball to his right, instead of having a go for goal himself, and Scholesy stooped low and twisted his body shape around in order to head home from just a few yards. It was a thoroughly deserved equaliser, as we'd been on top for most of the first half.

I'd just about calmed down when Rooney decided to show us all what he was made of, in first-half injury time. Scholes and Owen played a quick one-two, before the ginger one from Oldham touched it across to Rooney, who lashed it low into the net from about 21 or 22 yards out, just to the keeper's right. Cue delirium in the stands, as we all lost it.

The half-time break was a happy one and I spent a few minutes texting my brother and a mate back home, partly to make them feel jealous about my current location!

I'd been feeling confident all along to be honest and I felt that England had definitely been the better side in the first half. Paul and Met were sitting (or standing) closest to me and they were also extremely positive, especially about the boy wonder from Liverpool.

We had to wait until the 68th minute to see a bit more daylight between the teams, as the aforementioned Scouser bagged another one. He played a lovely one-two with Michael Owen close to the centre-circle and then took the ball on towards goal as he ran clear. As he got closer to the goal, he feigned to shoot to the keeper's left and then rolled the ball into the opposite corner for his fourth goal of the tournament. It really was a majestically composed finish for someone of his age.

Just a couple of minutes later, Sven brought Paul Scholes off and replaced him with Ledley King, which I thought was a bizarre, unnecessary, defensive move. Maybe Scholesy had picked up a knock, but why replace him with a defender? Sure enough, only a few minutes after the substitution, Croatia pulled one back from a corner when Tudor headed in after evading Ledley King's attempt at marking.

So it was nail-biting time again, which, to be fair, is not an unusual feeling for an England fan, but even so, I felt that we had been so much on top that anything other than a win would be an absolute travesty. The atmosphere inside the Stadium of Light was electric, as it had been all evening, but our mood was still generally positive and I sensed that most people around us expected more goals.

Frank Lampard obliged in the 78th minute, with the clinching goal. He drove towards the right hand side of the penalty area after receiving a pass inside from Beckham, and after dribbling around a desperate defender he drilled home a low shot from just inside the box, to make it 4–2. The feeling of relief was almost tangible and nobody could deny that it was well deserved, except perhaps a blindly biased Scottish or Irish supporter.

We were elated at the final whistle as it sent us through to the quarter-final, whereas the Croats had to book their plane tickets home. We stayed behind for a few extra minutes to savour the feeling and take a few more photographs, before we headed for the exits. It took ages to get on the metro as the station was absolutely packed, but I suppose that only irritates you when your team have lost.

We met up with Oz, Mo and the rest of the girls back in Rossio Square, and they all seemed, shall we say, well lubricated? Mo isn't the biggest of drinkers, but even she was in the thick of the singing, belting out that classic song known as "Rooney! Rooney! Rooney!" Oz's cheeks were red and his eyes had that glazed look, but that's usually a sign of a good time with him!

A very happy author after watching Croatia 2 England 4.

The pubs and bars around Rossio Square were packed full of celebratory England fans and the odd local, keen to be a part of it. The beers were flowing, yet again, and even Met wasn't too bothered about the price of the beer. Not for the first time though, we did end up heading for the funicular ride up the hill and into the Barrio Alto, scene of the Portuguese celebrations the night before. Our mate was there on the corner again, smiling as he observed more thirsty customers heading towards his street fridge. He distributed the one euro beers and we partied long into the night, singing and shouting, laughing and joking. I would have said dancing, but most of us had two left feet when it came to dance moves, so we just left that one alone!

The following morning started slowly. Very slowly. This was entirely due to the fact that almost all of us seemed to have a blinding hangover and a cow of a headache. Progress towards the cafe was slow, but life eventually returned to our fragile bodies as coffee and tea were consumed in vast quantities. The general consensus was that we'd done well, but more difficult games awaited us, such as the quarter-final against the hosts in just a few days time. Sadly for us, our flight back to London was booked for the afternoon of that quarter-final, so we'd end up watching it back in Twickenham, on the box. Work and financial commitments within our group meant that we didn't really have the option of staying and trying to acquire some tickets.

The plan for the day was to head up to the Parque das Nacoes, which translates as 'Park of Nations'. This area, just to the north-east from the city centre and adjacent to the river, is a leisure, office and eating complex, originally built for the Expo World Fair in 1998. The main attraction for us was the fact that it was UEFA's official 'Fan Zone' district for the duration of The European Championships, which meant all the games would be shown on huge screens in an area full of bars, restaurants and more bars. It sounded like a winner to us and the girls were also sold by the shopping opportunities and the large number of restaurants for eating at later on.

We got on the metro and hopped off at the Oriente station, which was very close to where the Fan Park had been set up. The huge Vasco da Gama bridge served as a stunning backdrop to the park, as did a large expanse of the River Tagus. The bridge also opened in 1998 and spans an extraordinary 10.5 miles, seven of which are over the river. I've yet to see a bridge that long anywhere else, so I did have a bit of a stare to be honest. I wouldn't want to use a cliché of course, but it really does take your breath away. Incredible feats of engineering like that have always impressed me.

We were all impressed with the park itself as well, as it was even better than we imagined it to be. We ended up having a brilliant day there and it wasn't really much of an anti-climax after the big game the night before.

The park wasn't really a park, more of a re-developed leisure and shopping zone, but there were so many things to see and do. There was a huge, white viewing tower and a cable car ride, hundreds of shops and restaurants, a huge aquarium called The Oceanario and lots of gardens and open spaces to promenade through, most of which had a pleasant river view.

We decided to go up in the viewing tower to get a great view across the river and the rest of the city, before a few of us also fell for the obvious tourist trap of the cable car ride, which ran parallel to the water's edge. Katie had me in stitches at the ticket office, as she finally plucked up the courage to use some of her Portuguese language skills that she had allegedly been practising for a couple of months beforehand. She approached the counter to buy two tickets for herself and Oz and came out with the classic, "Dos tickets please."

I couldn't resist taking the piss for at least three months after that. I suppose it was partly because it reminded me of my mate Scarecrow in Berlin, with his "Wunderbar" comment about the tomato soup.

Anyway, the cable car ride was great and we had an amazing view, even though I was happy to touch back down to earth at the other end. I'm not too good with heights you see. I mean, I've been up the Eiffel Tower in Paris a few times, but I daren't go to the top level, only the second stage.

After a quick beer we entered the UEFA fan zone for a look around. Getting into the zone required those of us with bags (the ladies) to acquiesce to a quick security search, though the cynic in me tended to think that this was less to do with safety than with their concern about fans bringing unofficial products into the official fan park, such as a rival drink company's bottle or a sneaky (cheaper) beer bottle, which might not have been the same as one of the official sponsors of the tournament. Seasoned football, cricket or tennis fans will know exactly what I'm talking about.

To be fair, the fan zone, once inside, was excellent. There were a few big screens up, ready to broadcast the day's games, but there were lots of other things to keep the punters entertained as well, even if much of it had corporate logos or branding all over it. There were a couple of five-a-side pitches, which we tried (and failed) to get on, as well as a penalty taking machine which measured how fast your kicks were, which was highly amusing, especially as Katie's kick was faster than her husband's. There were numerous food and drink outlets all serving fans a variety of temptations at inflated prices, but the number one attraction for me, by far, was the human table football game.

Picture a table football game in a pub, make it a hundred times bigger, attach real-life humans to the poles, or sticks, and then imagine inflatable goals and walls, and you've pretty much got it. It was absolutely hilarious. It took a while getting used to the fact that we could only slide across sideways, to the left or right, as opposed to forwards and backwards, but after five minutes or so the competitive edge definitely kicked in. We were one player short of even sides, so we roped in a Portuguese teenager who was hanging around, looking hopeful.

Paul went in goal for us whilst Kris and Cathy formed a formidable defensive line, whereas the goal scoring was left up to me and the local lad. The feeble opposition had Jim in goal, with Sue and Oz at the back. The laughably impotent strike force was Matt and Met, who wouldn't have scored in a brothel if we'd given them a few hundred euros each. Mo, Kate and Bev hung around at the side and spent most of their time laughing, or taking photographs. Let's just say the result was never in doubt.

Frustratingly, I've never seen one of these inflatables anywhere else since, so someone is missing a trick somewhere, as it was such a laugh. Maybe I should consider it as a future business idea. Charge a tenner a game for 15 minutes or so and I'm sure ten participants would pay a quid each for a go. I must look into that one.

We ended up watching the Denmark v Sweden game on the big screen, which finished 2–2. It wasn't too full so we could easily sit down and watch the game whilst helping ourselves to lots of 'official' beer. Several official staff members did their best to flog us some official mascot souvenirs, such as key rings or cuddly toys, but none of us had any need for a 'Kinas' mascot at home on the mantelpiece.

Human table football in Lisbon.

After the game we went for a bit of a stroll, or a 'promenade,' as it seems to be known in Mediterranean and Southern European areas. We had all our best gear on, obviously, which included a mixture of England, Nottingham Forest and Sheffield Wednesday shirts. Gok Wan would have been proud of us.

We eventually found a decent restaurant and settled down for a meal and rather too much vino tinto, but it was yet another bloody good night out. If anyone reading this has ever tried to find a restaurant which suits the taste buds of thirteen different people, I'm sure you will feel our pain, but we did eventually manage it, despite there being six ladies in our group! I'm joking girls!

The next day we caught a local train out to the beach resort of Estoril, which was only a short ride away. We ended up having a game of keepy-uppy on the beach, displaying all our Brazilian-esque skills for the locals to admire. Or something like that.

We flew back to England the day after, just as the city of Lisbon was gearing itself up for the huge game later that evening. You could say that we felt frustrated at having to leave, but most of us had commitments back home, so we sadly departed. Lisbon is a great city and I will definitely return at some point. Knowing me, it will probably be for a football game.

Those of us on the Heathrow flight got a taxi back to our place in Twickenham to watch the game. It all started so well, with a very early Michael Owen goal, but then the man of the moment, Wayne Rooney, decided to get himself injured. Our hopes seemed to fade with his departure, and although we clung on for a draw, we eventually, annoyingly, dispiritingly, managed to fail once again, at the dreaded penalty shoot-out stage.

To everybody's surprise, Greece went on to somehow win the tournament. I was glad, because it meant that I didn't have to see a gloating Christiano Ronaldo's face lifting the trophy. He's one of the best players I've ever seen, but boy, is he annoying, or what?

Greece didn't have our talented players, but they did have an incredibly tight defence, superb team spirit and a coach with a high level of tactical acumen. Luck also played an important part and they got it when it was needed. As an England fan, the fact that Greece won a trophy fills me with hope, because if Greece can do it, I'm sure that one day, England can somehow manage it too.

Chapter Four

UKRAINE 2012

By 2012, many more momentous events had changed my life. I was now living in Sydney, Australia and I had two wonderful little daughters, called Natalie and Emily. I'd been dragged over to Sydney by Mo, my wife, as the majority of her family lived there and as I'd been before for an extended holiday, I decided to give it a go.

Australia is a frustrating place to live for a football supporter, despite the obvious advantages of the climate, because most top quality football happens late at night or early in the morning, due to the time difference with Europe. Most of the time, I would find myself watching England games or Forest games at ridiculous times on the television and then having to go straight to work afterwards, which was just horrible. To me, football is best enjoyed with a beer, ideally in the afternoon or the evening. My football watching in Australia came with a coffee, breakfast and then a commute to work. I do follow one of the local teams in the A-League, known as Sydney FC, but it's just not the same, both in terms of quality and my level of interest, for obvious reasons.

In 2011, I made the decision to go to the European Championship Finals, which were due to be held the following year in both Poland and Ukraine. I sent out a number of emails to mates back at home in England, testing the water to see who was up for it. A few, such as Boro Graham and my brother Oz, were definitely up for it, whilst others such as Met and Paul showed interest as well. Things had changed for most of my mates as well, because most were now also married and some had kids of their own, together with demanding jobs. I was in the same boat, but I was determined to make this big trip, at great expense, partly because of the football isolation I was feeling down under. Sydney is a great place for many things, but for a passionate England supporter, it comes up short.

The draw for the finals was made very early in the morning in the Australian time zone, so I'd made plans to wake up early, watch the draw live and then immediately book flights and hotels, in the expectation that prices would skyrocket as soon as the airlines, hotel owners and tour operators had sussed out their own schedules. I'd told the boys back at home to make sure they were booking flights and hotels sharpish as well, but they were far too relaxed about it, presumably expecting to just organise a flight and hotel as and when they could be bothered to get round to it. I was booking for my brother and I, whilst Boro Graham was also on the ball and ready to move.

In all honesty, I think all of us wanted England to get drawn in Poland, as opposed to Ukraine, simply because we perceived that Poland was much easier, and therefore much cheaper, to get to. A few of the well-known budget airlines ran regular services to various Polish cities, and after googling the venues, we quite fancied the look of Krakow as a base. In the event of rip-off flight prices, we knew that Poland was still easy to enter from elsewhere, such as from across the border in Germany or the Czech Republic, so we had our fingers crossed for a convenient draw.

Of course, England got drawn in a Ukrainian group, along with Sweden, France and the Ukrainians themselves, with games due to be played in the capital, Kiev, along with Donetsk, in the far east of the country. I had planned and budgeted for a five-day trip from a base back in England, as I would be staying with family back home during a long holiday. Donetsk was out of the question, despite the fact that it was hosting an appealing tie for us, against the French. It would simply cost too much, and take too long to get there. I'd also looked online at both Kiev and Donetsk, and there was no comparison in terms of which venue looked the most aesthetically pleasing. It had to be Kiev.

Looking at the calendar, it suited me the most to fit in the Sweden game in the capital, so I quickly contacted all the boys back home to try and get them into gear.

After frantically searching for flights and hotels, I quickly realised that the hotels and airlines had already stepped up their prices in advance, before the draw had even been made. The hotels in particular were really taking the piss, charging around nine to ten times their usual rates. It was such big news that it even made most of the English newspapers. Radio talk show hosts and callers, television pundits and journalists alike were all united in their condemnation of the scandalous pricing strategies employed by hotel owners and most of the airlines. In short, they were having a laugh.

After a few hours searching online, I did eventually manage to find a flight and accommodation in Kiev at a price that I was prepared to pay. The cheapest flight I could get was with KLM, the Dutch airline, but it wasn't direct to Kiev: we'd have to change planes in Amsterdam first, which was a pain, but the price was much cheaper than any direct flight from England that I could find.

I couldn't track down a single decent looking hotel in the city centre that didn't have a stratospheric price tag attached to it. I had no option other than to start searching online for other types of accommodation and came across a few agencies that hired out apartments, usually to business executives who were in Kiev for a few days here and there. I ended up booking an apartment right in the centre of the city, which cost me £800 for four nights.. Now, that is a lot of money, but as we hoped to fill it with a group of lads, we thought we could manage for four nights by splitting the cost. Believe me, the majority of other prices were way in excess of that, so the location of the apartment itself was enough to tempt me into paying a more reasonable price. As it turned out, the location was as close to perfect as possible, but more about that later.

Sadly, the other lads had been too slow off the mark, and by the time they'd searched for flights a few days later, the prices had gone beyond ridiculous, so they had to back out. So, it was just going to be Boro Graham, Oz and myself on this trip. We still held out hope that some of the lads might surprise us in Kiev a few months later, as Matt and Lyndsay had once done in Greece a few years previously, but it wasn't to be on this occasion.

So, with flights and apartment booked, that just left the small matter of acquiring match tickets for the England v Sweden game. I wasn't a member of the England Fans set up anymore, as I didn't see the point, what with me living on the other side of the world, so I started searching for tickets online. The best price I was offered was on a ticket agency website, but before buying I decided to research as much as I could about that agency, which was called Ticketbis. From what I could find out, the feedback from other customers was reasonably positive, so I went for it and booked tickets with them several months in advance, from my home in Sydney. I did make a few phone calls to them (to Spain I think), just in case, checking on when my tickets would be delivered, but fortunately they did arrive at my parent's house in Sheffield in good time, which was a huge relief. I was spending so much money on this trip that I couldn't bear the thought of my tickets not being delivered. Anyway, all was well in the end, so the countdown began in earnest.

In the run up to the tournament, the BBC television programme 'Panorama' aired a story about violent, crazed, racist 'fans' in Ukraine who appeared to be more than willing to attack foreigners. One particularly disturbing scene, filmed in a stadium in the far east of the country, showed a few thugs randomly attacking a couple of fans sat watching a match, who appeared to be of Indian origin or similar. It was unpleasant to watch, without doubt, but then ex-England player Sol Campbell was interviewed and asked for his thoughts and opinions about Ukraine as a place. He came out with the infamous line about how he believed that some fans could be killed if they visited the country, because the hard-line, racist nutters over there would surely attack innocent foreigners like us.

Unfortunately for me, my dear mother was obviously watching the same show. Despite the fact that I am a fully grown adult with kids of my own, my mum was soon on the phone to me in Sydney.

"What the hell are you doing going to a place like that? It's not safe! I think you should cancel your flights."

I replied that far too much money had already been spent on the trip to back out now and besides, we were going to Kiev, the capital, not some backward provincial town over in the Eastern side of the country. Nonetheless, some of the reports in the media over the course of a few months were enough to make me feel a bit concerned, even though I was 100% positive that the Ukrainian authorities would strangle any kind of domestic problems at source, as the eyes of Europe were upon them. For a country like Ukraine, battling economic problems and the Soviet legacy, this tournament was a rare chance for them to show themselves off to the rest of Europe in the best possible light, so in my opinion, there was no way they would allow any kind of problem to occur, especially in terms of attacks on foreigners.

It seems strange writing this now in early 2014, because Ukraine is currently going through an awful period, what with riots, snipers, destruction and devastation in Kiev, and Russian influence in the Crimea region seemingly leading towards that particular peninsula joining the Russian state, against the wishes of the Ukrainian government. Back in 2012 though, Ukraine was trying its best to put on a show, and I was eagerly looking forward to the trip.

I thought it would be a good idea to try to find out some information from those on the ground, so to speak, so I contacted some British expats on a website forum specialising in Ukraine. The advice I received from a few fellow ex-pats based over there was fairly reassuring and positive, though they did suggest a few common sense safety measures like not dangling my camera around my neck and carrying two wallets, with one having only a small amount of cash in, just in case I had to give it up at knifepoint! Thankfully, the trip ended up being trouble free and very enjoyable, so I'd better get on with describing it.

With my daughters before the trip to Ukraine.

After a tedious few months at work, I was ready for the long flight from Sydney to Manchester, along with my wife and daughters. Anyone who has ever flown long haul with toddlers will know what a challenging experience that can be, but we made it without too much stress. The red wine helped though.

Despite being a naturalised Australian, my missus is more than happy to support England.

I spent an enjoyable few days with the family, back in Sheffield, before it was time to head back to Manchester with my brother, in order to get our flight to Kiev. We caught the National Express coach service over to Manchester and met Graham at the coach station, which was a good moment as I hadn't seen him for over a year. You may remember that he was an ex-flat mate of mine from my university days in Wolverhampton. Unsurprisingly, he was wearing a Middlesbrough shirt, as usual.

We had a few quick beers in the city centre and then decided to take in the Poland v Russia match in a Wetherspoons pub which happened to be close by. I eagerly grabbed a pint of Bombardier and settled down to watch the game, expecting to see some entertainment. There were quite a few Poles in there ready to cheer on their fellow countrymen, but what captured our attention was the rioting that had been taking place over in Poland, between Russian and Polish nutters earlier in the day. From what we could ascertain, it appeared to be instigated by the Russians, who were marching provocatively on a day of national importance to them. It didn't look good to be honest, so we were glad to be heading to a different country.

We left and caught the local train down to Manchester Airport station, where we had a hotel booked for the night. The flight time to Amsterdam was at stupid o'clock the next day, so we thought we might as well attempt to get some sleep, as opposed to coming over from Sheffield at a ridiculous hour.

The hotel was right next to the station, but we were hit with a problem as soon as we exited the platform. Road works and building works meant that the obvious direct route on foot to the hotel, which would have been about 200 yards at the most, was completely blocked off. The only way in appeared to be a long way around, through some road works, past some fences and piles of sand, take a quick left and then another left, and possibly then, we might have made the entrance. Taking into account the fact that it was about 10.30pm by this time and we'd had five or six beers in the city, we decided upon another course of action. There was a brick wall, approximately six feet high, which surrounded the hotel and its gardens. After a quick 'leg up' we spotted that there was a nice beer garden out the back of the hotel, which was being frequented by several patrons at the time. We looked at each other and instantly knew what we had to do. With a drunken laugh, we threw our bags over the wall, and then one-by-one, climbed and scaled the wall before jumping down over into the hotel premises.

We picked up our bags from the grass and tried to casually stroll towards the bar and the back entrance into the hotel, but a few guests had noticed us. One of them had been watching us the whole time and as we strolled past, he remarked with a smirk, "You wanna try walking in the front door lads," in a thick Mancunian accent.

We didn't get much sleep, because we had an airport transfer booked at a crazy time during the early hours. The minibus driver was suitably impressed when we told him we were off to Kiev for the football.

After a few badly needed coffees, we boarded the flight to Amsterdam, which was short and sweet. Schipol airport was very busy as we walked through the lounges and past the shops in our quest to transfer flights. We couldn't fail to notice hundreds and hundreds of Dutch supporters heading in the same direction as us, most of them wearing bright orange, as is their habit. Sadly for them, they ended up having a shocking tournament and would be heading back home within just a few days!

Eventually, after a pleasant flight, we touched down in Kiev. It took a while to find our driver, but we jumped into our pre-booked car and headed for the city centre. Our driver looked like someone you wouldn't want to mess with. He had the look and air of someone who used to be a KGB agent during Soviet times, or maybe that was just my imagination. Either way, he drove like someone who just didn't care about being pulled over by the police.

The road from the airport was big and wide and we saw little, other than lots of trees and many, many bus stops dotted along the route. As we got to the city's edge it was hard not to notice the large, ugly tower blocks that were ubiquitous. As we got closer to the centre itself, the buildings and standard of architecture in general started to improve somewhat, until we got stuck in several traffic jams of barely moving traffic. Eventually, we made it to our apartment, which just happened to be a couple of hundred metres from a main railway station and the UEFA fan zone, established along similar lines to the one we had visited in Lisbon. Talk about landing on our feet.

The apartment itself was decent enough, if small, but for three lads on a football trip to Eastern Europe, it would easily suffice. It was easy to see why the location was the main selling point of the place. The fan park was no more than a five minute walk away, along a road known as Khreschatyk, towards the Maidan, or Independence Square. Have a guess where we ended up spending the majority of our time? The Olympic Stadium, venue for the England v Sweden game, was a mere 15 minute stroll in the opposite direction. What a brilliant spot. I'd like to say that Oz and Graham congratulated me on my booking skills, but unfortunately I can't.

We were slightly apprehensive as we went out for a look around, mainly because we were unwilling to meet any Ukrainian nutters looking for a fight. As it happened, what we did find absolutely staggered us. Everywhere we went, everywhere we looked, were Swedes. Not the vegetable, but the Scandinavian people. Thousands of them, mostly covered from head to toe in Yellow and blue. In Lisbon a few years earlier it had been a city full of England fans, but here it was a city of yellow shirted Nordic people, often seen wearing plastic Viking helmets.

It turned out that Sweden were the only team in the competition who were based in the same city for all three of their group games, so thousands of Swedes had evidently come over for a fortnight's holiday in this city. Other countries, including England, had to travel to distant cities like Donetsk or Lviv for games, which were an absolute pain to get to, and made travel plans problematic and expensive. The Swedish flag was everywhere, draped over tents, shop windows and bar stools, as well as hanging from hotel and apartment balconies. What struck us the most over the next four days was how friendly and amiable they all seemed to be. Their spoken English was almost as good as ours, though better than Sven-Goran Eriksson's, and they were, almost without exception, friendly, chatty and curious. As we were mostly wearing England shirts during our trip, we were obvious targets for a conversation, and we were only too happy to stop for a chat and buy each other beers. The Swedish fans enamoured us so much during our trip that I think we all kind of took them to be our new second favourite team, purely because their fans were so brilliant.

With Oz and Graham in Kiev's fan zone.

The number of England fans present seemed to be significantly down on previous years, for a few reasons. Firstly, simply getting to Ukraine for most people was extremely expensive, even though it shouldn't have been. Secondly, the price of accommodation was prohibitive and thirdly, England had been hit hard by the financial recession, which meant that a large number of football fans had far less spare cash to spend on extravagances like this tournament. Finally, it should be admitted that most England fans didn't really expect this particular team to progress very far in the tournament, unlike Euro 2004 and the World Cup in 2006, when I think many England fans genuinely thought that we had a chance of winning it. Roy Hodgson had only been at the helm for a few months, after Fabio Capello's ignominious departure, so the general feeling was that he hadn't had enough time to shape and mould this mediocre bunch of players. I used those same four reasons to explain the lack of numbers from England when quizzed by a curious Israeli supporter in the fan park, but he wasn't convinced, as he'd seen huge numbers of England fans at most tournaments in recent memory.

When I say "lack of numbers" I should say that this was only in comparison to other recent tournaments. In fact, the English support was still probably one of the largest in Ukraine, but on this occasion, we just happened to be hugely outnumbered by Vikings in Yellow shirts. Not that we especially minded, and single man Graham had always been a fan of the blonde Swedish or Norwegian 'look' so he wasn't complaining.

Anyway, as we walked through the fan park, we noticed a huge sign which read 'Swedish corner' and sure enough, it was advertising a bar that happened to be full of yellow shirted football fans, all singing along to Abba and Roxette tunes. No, not really, I made that last bit up.

English fans were still few and far between on that first day as we explored the fan park, purely going on the football shirts we observed. The game itself was still a few days away though, so we contented ourselves with chatting to the Swedes and the locals. The beer tents serving imported beer were vastly overpriced, as expected, so we decided to make Lvivske our beer of the tournament, which was an acceptable local beer brewed in Lviv.

I couldn't help noticing that the local ladies were out in their droves, wearing their best dresses, mostly in heels, make-up caked on, whatever their age. It dawned on me that this was such a huge event for the country that no-one wanted to miss out on experiencing it, whether they were football fans or not. The novelty of having a large number of foreign tourists in town was probably too good an opportunity to pass up for most locals, even if their appearance at the fan park was driven solely by pure curiosity, in many cases.

From our point of view, there were two mouth watering games to look forward to later on, which were Denmark v Portugal and Holland v Germany, easily enough to excite any proper football fan. The Dutch were on the verge of elimination, whereas I felt bound to roar on Denmark, purely because I despised the gamesmanship of the Portuguese team, which was a shame as they were a talented bunch of players. Christiano Ronaldo is a superb footballer, but it's his attitude that turns me against him, as he's permanently whinging, moaning, diving and cheating, despite his skill and ability.

We left the fan zone for a while to explore some of the surrounding streets. We ended up sitting in a supposedly German bar in order to grab some liquid refreshment and a bite to eat, which ended up being a soggy version of sauerkraut, Ukrainian style. The beer was decent though, if again overpriced for this neck of the woods.

Graham spotted four vaguely attractive local ladies sat down on a park bench opposite our seats, so he decided to approach them and try his famous Geordie charm. Yes, I know Middlesbrough residents are not classed as Geordies, but it always served as an excellent wind-up whenever Graham was around. Anyway, I couldn't hear what he was saying to the girls, but in all honesty, it looked like he was crashing and burning to me, going on their facial expressions! He managed to squeeze onto the park bench and sat in the middle of them for a quick photo, but that was it. A definite fail on the first day for Graham, but then again, it was early.

Back in the fan zone later on, I thought I'd spotted Adrian Durham, the Talksport radio presenter, stood having a beer with a few mates. I pointed him out to Oz, who also listened to Talksport, but he had to confess that he didn't know what Adrian Durham looked like. I decided to try my luck so I barged into the middle of their conversation and interrupted them.

"Excuse me lads, sorry to butt in, but are you Adrian Durham?" I enquired of the red-haired one.

"Who?" he replied.

"Adrian Durham, the Talksport presenter, mad Peterborough fan," I said, suddenly starting to doubt my initial confidence, despite the beer.

They all cracked up laughing and started smacking the bloke on his back.

"Nah mate, we're all Pompey," one of them replied. "Never heard that one before."

Bugger. I could have sworn it was him. That's what Ukrainian beer does to your judgement I suppose.

We tried hard to find a decent spot to watch the games on the big screens, but the place was absolutely packed by early evening, so it was tricky. It was standing room only, much like being on an old style 'kop' apart from the fact that we could walk to a beer tent easily enough.

Sadly, the Danes went down 3–2 to Ronaldo's mob, and the Dutch lost to their historical rivals, the Germans, 2–1. There were hardly any supporters from any of those countries in the Kiev fan zone, but I suppose that's because they would have actually been in the stadium itself!

After popping into the 'official UEFA' souvenir shop on Khreshatyk for a quick nosey at all the tat on offer, we headed off back to the apartment for a few quiet ones and a decent night's sleep for once. We'd been up since 4.00am and we were absolutely knackered. Unfortunately, I ended up having to share a double bed with Boro Graham, as our Oz had already bagged the single bed. Those two must be the loudest snorers on the planet, especially our Oz, who sounds rather like a jet engine on take off. I've no idea how Katie puts up with it, but presumably she has a large supply of cotton wool.

The next morning we decided to pop over the Tarasa Shevchenko (Shevchenko Boulevard) to a posh-looking five star hotel, as we'd noticed their roof top bar from our apartment balcony and I thought we might get a decent view from the top. The doormen didn't bat an eyelid as three blokes walked in wearing England shirts and flip-flops and headed for the lifts. The hallway was very ornate and full of marble, so we did feel slightly underdressed, though we knew our nationality basically guaranteed us a safe passage upstairs to spend some money.

The view was indeed impressive, but the menu was crap and obviously overpriced, not that we had any plans to eat. We gave the foie gras, caviar and lobster a miss and opted for a bottle of champagne instead. Well, why wouldn't you?

We decided to be good tourists for much of the rest of the day and we had a good look around the city centre on foot. The Maidan, or Independence Square, was a lively place full of cafes and shops, some of which appeared to be temporary only, constructed purely for the tournament. Barely eighteen months after our visit, the square would be the scene of carnage, as pro-Western and pro-Russian locals fought and shot each other. Pro-Russian snipers hid in buildings and shot and killed a number of Ukrainian protesters who wanted the removal of the anti-Western President, Viktor Yanukovych. Back in 2012 however, all we saw were people overjoyed to be hosting a major international sporting tournament, and the locals mostly exhibited a mixture of pride and curiosity in their foreign guests, such as us.

A large, green, furry thing and a chunky, pink, alien thing accosted us in the square and they suggested that we might like to take photographs with them. The young people wearing the bizarre costumes must have been sweating inside them as it was a hot day, but they were eager to try out their English language skills on us. They were even more eager to try to persuade us out of a lot of hryvnia, the local currency, simply for their skills in posing for the camera. What their costumes had to do with the Euro 2012 Football Championships, I'm not entirely sure.

We headed up the hill towards the Sofiysky Sobor, which is an attractive old orthodox church, unlike anything we have in England. A couple of Stoke fans with backpacks approached us there, asking where the stadium was, so we pointed them in the right direction, though as they appeared to be newly arrived in the city, I hoped that they knew the game wasn't actually on until tomorrow night.

Now, I'm not really into exploring churches, but further along the road was an even more stunning building that demanded a closer inspection. The Andriyivska Tserkva (St Andrew's Church) really was beautiful and spectacular. It was predominantly painted in light blue and white, so Manchester City and Huddersfield fans would presumably have approved of the colour scheme, as well as the Baroque design and golden domes which topped off this amazing building. My guide book told me that it dated back to the 1750's, which impressed me further. If anyone reading this is ever in Kiev, I would definitely recommend that you give this orthodox church at least an hour of your time.

Just behind the church was a park which afforded us a good view over the Dnipro River and the rest of the city. We all grabbed an ice-cream from a scowling, frowning old woman who looked liked she'd spent most of her life queueing up for bread during the Soviet era. Her customer service skills were zero and she didn't seem remotely interested in serving three dodgy looking foreigners.

We eventually headed back down towards the Maidan and ended up in a sushi restaurant, as you do. Now, you may be thinking that Ukraine and sushi are not an obvious match, and you'd be right, but I think that was one of the main reasons we decided to enter, purely for the novelty factor. We ordered something from the menu and eagerly attacked it with chopsticks, which wasn't something we envisaged happening to us in this neck of the woods. It was bloody good though!

Graham wanted a look at the Lenin statue, which just happened to be within a stones throw of our apartment. There he was, standing proudly and dressed in a brown suit, on top of a black marble plinth. Lenin that is, not Boro Graham. Curiously, surrounding the statue were four bored looking soldiers. We found out later that soldiers are always stationed there, to ensure that the statue isn't vandalised or destroyed. Barely eighteen months later, it had been toppled.

The main game of note that evening was the Spain v Ireland clash, which we planned to watch in the fan park on the big screen. We fully expected the Irish to get hammered and the only question mark appeared to be related to how many goals the Spanish would get. We headed on down to the fan zone in the late afternoon and I shelled out some hryvnia on a small, official UEFA football, as our Oz had come up with an amusing idea. Remember that John Smith's television advert with Peter Kay in it? The one where they're all doing keepy-uppies or tic-tacs in the field, before Peter Kay lashes it into someone's back garden whilst shouting "Ave it," much like a centre-half for a pub team? Well, we were going to try to recreate that television advert in the fan zone and film it on our mobiles. Well, I would anyway.

Sushi in Ukraine? Yes, really.

There was just one slight problem: we weren't very good at the keepy-uppies. To be fair, it was because we were laughing hysterically like silly schoolboys, but we couldn't seem to manage more than five or six before it went pear-shaped. I had the camera phone in my right-hand, ready to film the action as the three of us attempted to show off our Brazilian style flair, but we couldn't do it for long enough. I blamed Graham for his performance, as he was much like Bambi on ice, wearing trainers. We were saved by a bloke wearing a Russia shirt, who asked if he could join us. He took it seriously, unlike us, and he was pretty decent. He was capable of quite a few tic-tacs on both feet and his thighs, so I resumed filming again. Finally, we made it. I started off with a few kicks, then volleyed it to Graham, who took it down on his chest and knocked it on to the Russian bloke. Russian bloke did a few keepy-uppies and passed it on to our Oz, who somehow kept the ball in the air, despite looking about as much at ease as an octopus on dry land, with arms and legs flailing and whirling. Suddenly, he belted it high into the sky and over the top of a beer tent whilst shouting "Ave it!"

I couldn't speak for a few minutes because I was laughing so much, but the Russian bloke didn't quite get the joke. He sprinted off after the ball and returned a few seconds later with a very confused expression on his face. Fortunately, I'd captured it all on my phone for the viewing pleasure of the lads back at home. Well, we thought it was amusing anyway.

I went off to get another round in from one of the beer tents and the queue was extremely long, as usual. By the time I got back, I found Graham chatting to a couple of girls, who turned out to be locals. Marianna and Lilyu were no doubt practising their English skills, but I was sure Graham was looking for a positive result. Oz came back from the toilets laughing, as he'd just witnessed a Swedish bloke with a beard dressed up as Goldilocks attempting to unzip himself in the urinals, which was apparently proving difficult for the poor chap!

We got chatting to another Swedish bloke who was very amiable and friendly, but we couldn't pronounce his name properly, so we just went with 'Thor,' which he found funny, fortunately. He looked more like a rugby player than a football fan, as he could easily have passed as a loose head prop. Fortunately, he didn't ask us to swap shirts, as many foreign fans had done, because his shirt would have looked like a tent on any of us, whilst he would probably have had to wear any of our shirts as a bandana.

Getting on famously with the Swedes in Kiev!

Thor came with us towards the big screens with his mate and we settled down to watch the Spanish thrash the Irish. As expected, the Irish defence proved no match for the Spanish attack and the goals started to fly in. During the latter stages of the game, a few raindrops started to fall on us as the sky darkened considerably. Within a few minutes the heavens had opened and it started absolutely bucketing it down. The rain was so heavy that only a passionate Spanish fan would have stayed to watch the end of the one-sided match, and I couldn't see any of those. We all sprinted for the buildings which surrounded Independence Square and the little areas of shelter offered there. As hundreds and hundreds of fans were all doing the same thing, I got separated from Graham, Oz and Thor.

I ended up trying to keep dry under a very small awning that sprouted from the side of an old, grey, dirty looking building. I spotted another bloke with an England shirt on, so I started up a conversation with him. Roger was in his fifties I'd say, and was travelling on his own, surprisingly. He was a big Bristol Rovers fan from Cheltenham and he mentioned that he'd been looking forward to this tournament for a while, but unfortunately, none of his usual travel companions could make the trip, so he'd obviously thought 'sod it' and decided to come anyway. Fair play to the fella I thought.

After the rain eased off slightly, Graham finally answered his phone and we agreed to reconvene in the bar of a nearby five star hotel, despite the fact that we were all soaked to the skin. I suppose that was a good enough reason to persuade ourselves that we deserved another beer!

I dragged Roger along as he was on his own and I thought he could probably do with meeting some more fans. Thor had come along as well and impressed us with his ability to speak in our own language. He was certainly able to structure a sentence much better than one or two players and managers at home that I could easily think of!

Roger ended up sleeping on a chair in our apartment, because he told us that as he'd booked late, the only accommodation he'd managed to find was a dodgy little room in a dodgy little suburb, way out in the distant suburbs of the city. When he described the tall, dark, grey, tower blocks that littered 'his' suburb, as well as the groups of bored, hooded youths who loitered around there, I thought I'd do him a favour by offering him a free night at our place, which was only a five minute stroll away. He'd still have to go back tomorrow to get changed and pick up his match ticket, but it sounded much better for him in the middle of the day than at this time of night. Fortunately, he didn't snore, unlike the other two legitimate guests. Anyway, when abroad in unfamiliar territory, England fans should always look after fellow England supporters!

The following day was match day and our apartment reeked of excitement and anticipation. Well, not really. It reeked alright, but that was our Oz's feet and his dodgy digestive system. In reality, we all awoke with a cow of a hangover and coffee was required by all in order to get us back into the land of the living. Roger thanked us profusely and made his way to the station so that he could get back to Hackney. Well, it sounded as bad as Hackney anyway, as opposed to one of the less salubrious suburbs of Kiev.

England's opening game in Donetsk against France a few days earlier had been reasonably encouraging, despite the fact that few people seemed to have any faith in this particular team. I'd watched that game in The Leadmill, easily the best nightclub in Sheffield, which had opened its doors early to accept the hordes of fans. Paul, Matt, Oz, Met, Woody and I had watched Lescott head England in front from a Steven Gerrard free-kick, but sadly, the French equalised later through Nasri, and it ended 1–1. If Milner had slotted home when faced with an open goal from a tight angle, we would have been in a better position, but the French didn't trouble us too much, apart from one incident which needed a great Joe Hart save from a close range French header.

England's opponents for our big match, Sweden, had been a bit of a bogey team for us in recent years, as we hadn't beaten them for decades until a friendly win at Wembley the year before. We were feeling pretty confident though on this match day and we definitely had a spring in our step as we left the apartment, all kitted out in the same white England home shirt.

We walked the streets for a bit and had a bit of lunch in a small Ukrainian cafe, where the service was snail-like, not for the first time on this trip. During a brisk walk to a much-loved pub, Graham suddenly darted into a mini-supermarket without warning and reappeared a few minutes later with what could only be described as a blow-up Fred Flintstone club, complete with little silver spikes. He had also acquired a blue and yellow hat, which had the same shape and style as the one worn by Captain Pugwash in the 70s and 80s. I tried to point out to Graham that his lovely hat was in the colours of today's opponents, but I don't think it registered with our Geordie friend, who seemed to be off on another planet for a while. To the best of my knowledge, he doesn't have a taste for any illicit drugs, but maybe he'd had a sneaky quick one that morning without letting us in on it. Either way, that bloody Fred Flintstone club finished up appearing in most of our photographs on that day, but I'm still not sure why. Supporting Middlesbrough can do strange things to your mind it seems.

The walk to the stadium would have taken about fifteen minutes if we'd marched directly there, but as we were in no rush, we decided to take in as much as we could, because the road to the ground was absolutely packed with football fans. Most of these fans were Swedish, but there was still a decent amount of both England and Ukraine fans, out mingling, swapping scarves, posing for photographs and engaging in the odd sing-song. The Ukrainians were also playing today in the earlier game, over in Donetsk, so most of the locals who were out seemed to slowly head for the bars as soon as kick-off time approached for their game against the French.

We couldn't physically get inside any of the pubs or bars as they were all packed for the Ukraine game, but fortunately, it was possible to get served whilst standing in the street, from a side bar. The one we chose also happened to have a decent view of a television, so we happily stood and chatted, whilst watching the game. A huge storm over in Donetsk actually delayed the game, as what looked like a year's amount of rain quickly deluged the pitch, leaving most areas waterlogged, including the stands in the stadium. After a while, the game did get under way, but conditions looked atrocious from where we were standing.

Dark clouds were also visible on the horizon in Kiev and I suddenly had a nightmare vision of the England game being cancelled due to a flooded pitch, much like the classic '*Likely Lads*' episode on television in the 70s, when England were flooded out in Bulgaria. I had spent some serious money on getting here to Kiev, all the way from Australia, and I certainly wasn't going to accept a postponement! As it happened, the rain did come to Kiev, but not until much later at night, when we got soaked bar hopping after the game had finished.

We left the bar after the game had finished with a defeat for the locals. As we walked towards the stadium, we passed a bar called 'Lucky Pub' (what imagination!), which was covered in England flags, and I couldn't help but notice two of the more unusual St George Crosses. One of them had the legend 'Cote d'Azur BCFC' written across the middle, with both the England and Birmingham City badges on display, whilst another proclaimed 'Chesterfield LTFC', which left me wondering how big the Luton Town fan club was in North Derbyshire. Sadly, our infamous 'Goldie' flag was no more, having slowly died a death due to the ravages of time, as well as Kris and Ant's complete inability to look after it properly!

Kick-off approaches in Kiev. Graham still had his Fred Flintstone club, despite our attempts to accidentally lose it.

We eventually made it to The Olympic Stadium after posing for innumerable photographs with friendly Swedes and locals, who obviously all wanted three handsome English chaps to feature in their photo albums for years to come.

From the outside, the ground looked impressive. A huge poster of the European Championship trophy was the centrepiece, staring straight at us from the main entrance. We had to pass through three security cordons before finally being allowed in to the stadium. The first thing we saw was a group of England fans (who turned out to have an Indian background) proudly holding up a huge St George Cross which read 'Are you watching Sol Campbell?' in huge letters across the middle, which was a blatant reference to the ex-England defender's recent appearance on *Panorama*. Of course, we had to go and have a chat with them.

They turned out to be Tottenham and Luton fans and they'd travelled a fair bit watching England in previous years. They absolutely slated Sol Campbell for his ridiculous comments about what awaited any black or Asian fans who dared to travel to Ukraine. They told us they were having the time of their lives and had been treated perfectly normally ever since they had arrived in the country, and they were openly vocal about that. I just hope their great flag did get noticed by the television cameras.

I lined up for about ten minutes at one of the stadium bars to buy three overpriced Carlsberg beers, only to then be told, after my purchase, that they were alcohol free. I was absolutely gutted. There can't be many things worse than alcohol free beer, except perhaps caffeine-free coffee, both of which completely miss the point, don't they? Sadly, all the beer available in the stadium was alcohol free, which had never occurred to us as a possibility. Suffice to say that when we had downed our tasteless liquid, we didn't bother with any more.

The view from our seats, when we had finally found them, was impressive. We were positioned in the top tier, above the main 'official' England support. Perhaps not surprisingly, given the evidence of our own eyes over the previous few days, we were hugely outnumbered inside the stadium by the Swedes, which in recent years had become a rarity for England's amazing travelling support. The obvious disparity in numbers wasn't helped by the fact that all the seats in the stadium were yellow, which is the colour that both Ukraine and Sweden play in.

I couldn't see the Sol Campbell flag anywhere, but then I probably wasn't in the best place to view the England support, as I was sat above them. Filling up the seats around us were mainly locals actually, which left me wondering exactly where Ticketbis had picked up our three tickets from.

There were lots of England flags in Kiev, but nowhere near as many as in Lisbon, eight years previously.

When the teams came out, I was disappointed to see that England were wearing their dark blue away shirt, which for me, is a silly colour for England to play in. White and red are our national colours, so our home shirt should be white and our away shirt red, in my opinion.

The opening was fairly cagey, as both teams checked each other out. Scott Parker was the first to really trouble Andreas Isaksson, their goalkeeper, with a decent effort from around 25 yards out. We only had to wait 23 minutes for the breakthrough goal though, as Steven Gerrard whipped in a high ball from the right-hand side and Andy Carroll leapt like a salmon, way above the Swedish defenders, to powerfully head home into the corner of the Swedish goal. I was already out of my seat as I saw the ball coming over and Carroll towering majestically over Olof Mellberg, the ex-Villa centre-half.

The rest of the first-half was fairly comfortable for England, with the main highlight being the continued baiting of Zlatan Ibrahimovic, easily Sweden's best player, with chants emanating from the England support of "You're just a shit Andy Carroll, shit Andy Carroll, you're just a shit Andy Carroll!" which was mainly a reference to both striker's dodgy long hair and huge frame. Ibrahimovic was and is a quality player, but at that time, in 2012, he had rarely produced anything of note when playing against England or English club sides in Europe. Sadly, the following season, he produced the best goal I've ever seen during a friendly in Stockholm between the two countries, when he scored an incredible over-head kick from way out of the penalty area, after Joe Hart had got caught way out of his goal. The technique and skill shown in that goal was incredible, despite England's defensive failings in that particular game.

Anyway, back to Kiev. England started the second half sluggishly, despite being in a commanding position, and after 49 minutes, the Swedes equalised. Andy Carroll clumsily gave away a free-kick about 25 yards out, which Ibrahimovic took. His shot was blocked by the wall, but the ball rebounded out to the Swedish striker, who volleyed it back into the penalty area as the English defence rushed out. Unfortunately, Olof Mellberg was left completely unmarked and he had enough composure to turn the ball home, with Glenn Johnson just failing to keep to keep the ball from crossing the line.

Sweden v England at Euro 2012.

It's fair to say that I was slightly displeased at this point, but my irritation turned to apoplectic rage just ten minutes later, when the same player scored again for the Swedes. The goal came from another free-kick, as the ball was swung over from the left-hand side of the pitch by Larsson, and was headed home by the completely unmarked Mellberg from six yards out. England had left the same player completely unmarked twice in ten minutes, and this smacked of poor defensive organisation to me.

I was absolutely spitting blood. I turned to Oz and said, "I haven't come all the way from bloody Australia to watch this crap!" Oz just shook his head in disbelief, whilst Graham just looked on impassively. It wasn't the first time that us England fans had seen a defensive collapse of course, but I really didn't need it right at that moment, especially as I'd shelled out hundreds and hundreds of pounds and dollars!

Fortunately, England slowly started to wake up again and the rest of the second half was superb entertainment. Glenn Johnson whipped in a tasty looking cross from the right and John Terry's downward header from six yards was miraculously turned over the bar by Isaksson, which had me shouting out in frustration, high in the stands above that goal.

Shortly afterwards, England were level. Ashley Young sent in a corner that was headed out by a Swedish defender in the direction of Theo Walcott, who then drilled it home from approximately 25 yards, via a slight deflection. Cue elation in the stands, as we jumped up and celebrated a deserved leveller.

For some reason, the deflection reminded me of a Sunday league game I once played in, for the might Rollneck Rings FC in 1992. I was usually a centre-forward for the team, but as we had a lot of absences, sickness and injuries, I was asked to cover as centre-half in a cup game against a team six divisions above us. At that time, our team had only just started up and we had a few, ahem, technically challenged players in our side, along with several who were far more comfortable raising a glass in a pub than they were when asked to run around for a bit. We suitably lost 16–0 and I was accused by the lads of scoring four own goals, when the reality was that they were all deflections, as I worked hard to close down an opening, much like that Swedish defender in Kiev! Anyway, just to redress the balance a bit, just two years later, I scored an incredible 42 goals in one season, which earned me the Player's Player of the Season trophy, which I don't like to talk about much. Just ask the lads in The Rag!

Anyway, back in Kiev, England were slowly starting to turn the screw and went 3–2 ahead after 78 minutes when Danny Welbeck scored a superb goal. Theo Walcott stormed into the inside-right channel and pulled the ball back across the edge of the six-yard box, and Welbeck somehow twisted his body to flick the ball into the net with the inside of his right foot, despite facing away from goal. It was a really classy finish and he headed off towards the English support, arms aloft in celebration.

I was cheering and shouting so much that I lost my voice for a while. It took at least two hours afterwards for my throat to stop croaking after all the adrenalin had poured through my body and the guttural screams had eased off. I also gashed my shin against the back of the seat in front after jumping up when Welbeck scored. I'd done exactly the same thing at Wembley during the Euro 96 game between England and Scotland. When Alan Shearer's header put us 1–0 ahead, I jumped up behind that same goal and smashed my right shin to pieces against the chair in front of me. Wembley wasn't renowned for leg room at that time, but the pain was worth it of course!

Steven Gerrard almost claimed a fourth for England later on, as the Swedes pushed up, leaving a few gaps, but it wasn't to be. The celebrations were loud and clear amongst the English support, whilst the Swedes drifted off back into the city, aware that they were now out of the tournament.

Sweden 2 England 3.

I was over the moon of course, but boy, I needed a beer. Why do England have to put us through those kinds of emotions during every tournament? We headed off out of the stadium after engaging in some celebratory singing with the rest of the England fans. We found a bar close to the ground that had some England fans in, so we entered and ordered six beers, as we were very thirsty! Graham was happy, as a few other Middlesbrough fans were congregated on the table next to us, so he got busy discussing smog, smoke, pollution, heavy industry and high unemployment levels in his home town.

I was trying to relax and enjoy the moment, but my stomach was having other ideas. You know that feeling when you've just got to go? I had no option other than to walk very briskly towards the toilet, which fortunately, did actually have a lock that worked, unlike so many others. Put it this way, I'm sure I lost a few kilograms in weight during those few moments on the loo! It must have been something I'd eaten, or then again, it could have been the horrific alcohol-free beer that we were served in the stadium!

We eventually moved back towards the city centre after most of the crowd had dispersed and we somehow found ourselves crammed into one of the tiniest bars I'd ever been in, mainly just so that we could escape the rain which had started to fall on the city. We didn't especially care about the weather though, as we were all feeling elated after the game. Next up for England were the hosts, but for now, it was simply time to celebrate.

The next bar we found was much better, because it was absolutely packed with England fans in a happy mood, as well as a few Swedes and Ukrainians who were just out for a good time. Graham decided to get the shots in, as he is prone to doing, so before we knew it we were sat at a table necking a variety of foul smelling offerings.

Walking back to the apartment was a bit of a struggle later on, though Oz agreed to swap his England shirt with a Swede offering his bright yellow top in exchange. I've no idea to this day whether or not our Oz has actually worn that shirt ever since, but it was a decent souvenir of a great trip.

The Beckett brothers in Kiev, Ukraine.

We entered our apartment building and sat and had a couple more beers together, before I went onto the balcony for a quick look at the rain. I noticed a shadowy figure, dressed all in black, trying to huddle up underneath a park bench opposite our room, across the street. The rain was pouring down and this poor bloke, presumably homeless, was really open to the elements. I couldn't help but watch him turn on his side, then his back, then his front, as he somehow attempted to sleep. I'd never want to be homeless, but I certainly wouldn't want to be homeless in an ex-Soviet state such as this. Poor sod.

The next day didn't really start for us until lunchtime, for obvious reasons. The day of the match had been a very long one, but ultimately a very satisfying one. We went for a stroll along Khreschatyk, to clear our heads a bit, but Oz couldn't resist the hole-in-the-wall bar. One magnificent Kiev attraction for us was the fact that occasionally, we'd come across little more than a sliding window in a wall, from which draught beer on tap was served, in plastic take-away 'glasses' at cheap prices. It reminded me of the bloke selling beer in the street in Lisbon, apart from the fact that this beer was served from an open window. What a shame it is that our nanny state won't trust our people to enjoy this kind of convenience. In reality, these kinds of premises were tiny little corner shops, serving little other than basic foods and a few drinks, but we loved them. Imagine being able to get a take-away draught beer back at home from a street kiosk or your local newsagent's window!

We saw Greece surprisingly knock the Russians out of the tournament later in the evening, and then Poland, the other tournament hosts, exited their own competition after losing to a Czech team who happened to hit form on the day. England had to play our hosts, the Ukrainians, in just a few days time. We had to return to England for family reasons, so I ended up watching that game in a local pub back in Stocksbridge, close to my parents' house. Anyway, as we waited to change planes back in Amsterdam, I remember having a conversation with a Dutch barman, who tried to tell me that England had been lucky against the Swedes! I wasn't having that! I don't know what game he'd been watching, but apart from the opening fifteen minutes of the second half, England had always been the better team and created the most chances. I presumed he was just jealous, because the Dutch had been miserable in the tournament, going home early after three failures.

The Ukraine versus England game wasn't a classic by any means, but as I watched from a distance, back in Sheffield, a clearly unfit Wayne Rooney bagged the only goal of the game from close range, which was enough to knock the hosts out and send us through to the quarter-finals. There were a couple of scares, such as a John Terry goalline clearance that may, or may not have crossed the line, but overall, I felt we deserved the win and the chance to progress.

I ended up watching the quarter-final against Italy at my mate Tord's house, in Surrey. Tord isn't his real name, but I've always called him Tord since we teamed up together to run a boys and girls school football team in a place called West Molesey, which is near Hampton Court, between 2003 and 2005. As I was the 'official' manager of the team, he called me 'Sven' for a joke, after the current England manager of the time, Sven-Goran Eriksson. Sven's assistant with the England team at that time was his fellow Swede, Tord Grip, hence the name for my assistant, Andy.

England held their own for the first half and Rooney had a decent chance to grab a goal, but 0–0 was an acceptable score going in at half-time. The second half was a totally different ball game though, as Italy dominated. Our players seemed as if they were running through quicksand and they simply couldn't get hold of the ball, or keep it. To me, our players looked exceptionally fatigued, and the midfielders and strikers just disappeared. The defence were heroic though, as they kept the Italians out, with John Terry being a standout as man of the match for us. We somehow held on for a 0–0, despite being comprehensively outplayed, yet I admired our solid defensive work under pressure.

So we were left to face another penalty shoot-out, which history shows is usually a disaster for England. We have only won one penalty shoot-out in a major finals, and that one was at home in London, in 1996 against the Spanish. Other than that, we have had disasters and calamities and periods of national mourning after shoot-outs against the Germans in 1990, the Germans again in 1996, Argentina in 1998, Portugal in 2004 and then Portugal again in 2006. Surely then, this time, in 2012 against the Italians, it had to be our turn, didn't it?

Apparently not. By the so-called 'Law of averages' we should have won this one, surely? Unfortunately, Italy held their nerve and we did not, once again. Why do our players seem to crumble under extreme pressure, whereas others, such as Andrea Pirlo in this instance, rise to the challenge? Pirlo's cheeky, cocky, little lob of a penalty showed his confidence in his own ability, but England's penalty takers, when it came to the crunch, weren't quite good enough, yet again.

To say I was devastated would be an understatement and I lost the power of speech for about an hour or so afterwards. I simply couldn't think of anything to say that hadn't already been said a million times by my fellow countrymen and women. Despite being outplayed, we were so close, once again, to the semi-finals. Our penalty shoot-out record has gone way beyond a bad joke now and the problem is definitely a psychological one.

At the time of writing this, in early 2014, I hear that the current England manager Roy Hodgson has decided to take an expert in Sports Psychology with him to the World Cup Finals in Brazil, which in my opinion, can only be a good thing.

Epilogue

Following England abroad is an amazing, exciting, energising experience, as well as an opportunity for some 'male bonding' and the chance to see more of the world. That's not to say that there aren't a lot of travelling female supporters, because there are, but the majority are most definitely male, as backed up in my own individual case.

I've had some of the best experiences of my life watching football, even if I include those times watching my club team, Nottingham Forest. Unfortunately, there have also been more than a few disappointments over the years, which non-football fans can't quite seem to understand, or fully appreciate. With England, the penalty shoot-out defeats against Germany in 1996 and Argentina in 1998 in particular, still haunt me to this day, as the frustration of being an England fan shows no sign of coming to an end, just yet. To balance that out a little, the joy of beating Scotland 2–0 at Wembley during Euro 96, or the 4–1 massacre of the Dutch during the same tournament evoke many happy memories. Then there was the 5–1 win over Germany in Munich, or the 1–0 win over Argentina during the World Cup in Japan, or the 4–1 away win in Croatia, or even the classic 3–0 win over the Poles during the Mexico 86 World Cup, all of which were great victories.

England ARE a very good national team, but we haven't been able to match the heights attained by some of our European rivals, such as Germany, Italy, France and Spain, which are countries we often compare ourselves to, because of their football histories and populations, both of which provide reasons for English fans to feel that we should be doing much better.

I have tickets for the England v Peru friendly international in late May 2014, which is a warm up game ahead of the World Cup, being staged this year in Brazil. Work and family commitments prevent me from going to Brazil, but I'll be watching every single game from pubs in places such as Sheffield, Nottingham and Hastings. Most fans seem to think that the current England team under Roy Hodgson, isn't quite good enough to progress far in Brazil, but this lack of expectation, which is rare in England, certainly amongst tabloid journalists and headline writers, could just do the players a favour for once, and maybe allow them to play with less fear this time around.

I've been fortunate to travel to many countries around the globe watching football and I sincerely hope that these kinds of opportunities continue to present themselves to me, even as I enter a new period in my life, which is that of a father. Rest assured, I am already doing more than my best to ensure that my young daughters, Natalie and Emily, grow up to be England fans and who knows, maybe even England players of the future, for the ladies team! We've already been out in the back garden practising taking penalty kicks.

Glenn Beckett
Sydney, April 2014.

6737235R00083

Printed in Great Britain
by Amazon.co.uk, Ltd.,
Marston Gate.